OBSTRUCTION OF JUSTICE

THE SEARCH FOR TRUTH
ON CANADA'S HIGHWAY OF TEARS

Ray Michalko

Red Deer Press

OBSTRUCTION
OF JUSTICE

THE SEARCH FOR TRUTH
ON CANADA'S HIGHWAY OF TEARS

Published in·Canada by Red Deer Press,
195 Allstate Parkway, Markham, ON L3R 4T8

Published in the United States by Red Deer Press,
311 Washington Street, Brighton, Massachusetts 02135

www.reddeerpress.com   rdp@reddeerpress.com

10 9 8 7 6 5 4 3 2 1

Red Deer Press acknowledges with thanks the Canada Council for the Arts, and the Ontario Arts Council for their support of our publishing program.

We acknowledge the financial support of the Government of Canada.

Funded by the Government of Canada

 Canada Council   Conseil des arts
for the Arts   du Canada

 ONTARIO ARTS COUNCIL
CONSEIL DES ARTS DE L'ONTARIO
an Ontario government agency
un organisme du gouvernement de l'Ontario

Library and Archives Canada Cataloguing in Publication

Michalko, Ray, author
Obstruction of justice : the search for truth on Canada's Highway of Tears / Ray Michalko.

ISBN 978 - 0 - 88995 - 545 - 5 (paperback)

1. Murder—British Columbia. 2. Murder—Investigation—British Columbia.
3. Missing persons—British Columbia. 4. Native peoples—Crimes against—British Columbia. I. Title.

HV6535.C32B75 2016   364.152'309711   C2015-908663-9

Publisher Cataloging-in-Publication Data (U.S.)

Names: Michalko, Ray, author.

Title: Obstruction of justice : the search for truth on Canada's Highway of Tears / by Ray Michalko.

Description: Markham, Ontario : Red Deer Press, 2016. |Summary: Author Ray Michalko, an ex-RCMP, has spent the last 10 years investigating a series of murders and missing persons along Highway 16, a section of the Trans-Canada Yellowhead Highway.

Identifiers: ISBN 978-0-88995-545-5 (paperback)

Subjects: LCSH: Murder – Canada – Investigation. | Obstruction of justice – Canada. | BISAC: TRUE CRIME / Murder / General.
Classification: LCC HV8079.H6M334 |DDC 363.259523 – dc23

Text and cover design by Tanya Montini
Front cover images courtesy of Shutterstock and 123rf.com
Printed in Canada

Dedicated to Canada's murdered
and missing women
and their families.

In memory of my late wife Shirley,
for her love, unwavering support
and understanding.

CONTENTS

PREFACE

It was the summer of 1967. I had recently graduated from RCMP training and was finally allowed to work alone. We didn't have bulletproof vests in those days; I didn't need one. After years of waiting, I was a member of the greatest police force in the world. Bullets would literally bounce off my chest. As I proudly drove my police car through the quiet Manitoba countryside, a vast patchwork of farmer's fields and shallow gullies peppered with spruce and white birch, a call came over the police radio instructing me to be on the lookout for a six-year-old Aboriginal boy. Just a few days earlier he had run away from Birtle Indian Residential School, southwest of my detachment's policing area. As I acknowledged receipt of the call I suddenly saw the boy walking down the shoulder of the highway. Excited because I was about to solve my very first case, I raced down the road toward the kid.

The frightened runaway was slightly off course but determined to complete his trip home. He told me he had been taken from his family home on a Native reserve, which I calculated to be several hundred miles north, and sent to the residential school. Many years later I learned that the old brick school that had been located on a hill overlooking Birtle was opened as a dedicated residential school in 1894, and finally closed in 1972.[1] The boy told me he hated his new school and, as he used his dirty shirtsleeve to wipe away the tears that were rolling down his cheeks, said he really missed his mom and dad and begged me to let him go. For a split second I seriously considered his request, but realizing that he was far from his family and that many bad things could happen out here on the road, I changed my mind. After all, what could be so bad about going to school in Birtle? I did what I was paid to do and arranged to meet a member from a neighbouring detachment to begin a shuttle that would eventually return the boy to his studies.

I have since forgotten the kid's name, but after reading Arthur Fourstar's account of his experience at the Birtle Residential School, I couldn't help but worry that I might have caused the runaway the same kind of suffering. Fourstar recalls being at home with his mother, his father off fighting in the Second World War. One day two men, one of which was a Mountie, burst into their home uninvited. The Mountie grabbed his mother while the other hauled Arthur outside and put him in the car. Arthur said that this was "when the darkness began." Children that got caught running away from residential schools were "undressed and whipped in front of the other students who were forced to watch." Arthur said "he got a lot of beatings."[2]

Residential schools had their origins in the pre-Confederation period and were eventually phased out in the 1980s. They were administered by a number of religious denominations in partnership with the federal government. It is estimated that by the 1980s, when most schools were closed, about 150,000 First Nations, Métis and Inuit students had passed through the system. These children had been taken from their families for reasons other than "education." As John A. Macdonald, our first prime minister told the House of Commons in 1883: "When the school is on the reserve the child lives with its parents, who are savages; he is surrounded by savages, and though he may learn to read and write his habits, and training and mode of thought are Indian."[3]

In 1927, the RCMP and local police departments were appointed truant officers for the schools. I guess that's where I came in that day, policing the runaways, oblivious like so many of us were, to what was really going on in those schools.

Years later, now that I am aware of the residential-school disgrace, I'm haunted by the little boy I spent so little time with all those years ago. Sometimes I still wake not knowing if he made it through his school experience unharmed or if I am responsible for returning him, like Arthur Fourstar, to the darkness that began when he was torn from his family.

Many new RCMP recruits like me were sent directly from training to police Western Canadian towns that had—or were near—large populations of Aboriginal people. Yet we never received any instruction on First Nations culture or how to best interact with Indians, the label we used in those days. Nor were we told about the residential schools, which had been filled with kids who had, in many cases, been forcibly removed from their homes with the help of the RCMP. In fact, a First Nations friend living in Northern British Columbia told me the Dakelh people refer to the RCMP as *Nilhchuk-un*, meaning "those who take us away," a title that the independent international organization, Human Rights Watch, used in its 2013 report, *Abusive Policing and Failures in Protection of Indigenous Women and Girls in Northern British Columbia, Canada.*

I knew nothing about Aboriginal people prior to joining the RCMP so I had no idea that just a couple of years before joining the force and arriving in Manitoba, the body of an Aboriginal girl was found at the bottom of a cement staircase that led to the basement of her foster mother's home in Rossburn, a couple hours southwest of my new home. Even though there was no evidence of disease, and her numerous injuries couldn't be explained by an accident, the cause-of-death was determined to be just that, accident or disease, and this was willingly accepted by the RCMP. Thirty years later, Manitoba's chief medical examiner, Dr. Peter Markesteyn, said that based on reasonable medical probability, the girl had been a victim of homicide, her injuries consistent with abuse.[4]

Nor did I ever imagine that decades later, the "I'm not a social worker" attitude I had learned as a police officer tasked with policing Aboriginal people—an attitude adopted from my crime-fighting predecessors—would still be widespread in Western Canada. For example, in Saskatchewan, a 2004 Justice Reform Report identified a sixty-year-old Aboriginal woman with a drinking problem who, sometime prior to 1994, had been arrested by the Mounties a mind-boggling 897 times. When asked why, the police said: "We only pick people up. We're not social workers." Incidentally, the judge said: "All I determine is guilt. I don't care about what else happens." And the prosecutor said: "I don't know what the police do, but I only deal with the files that are given to me on court day."[5]

It's true police officers are not social workers, but they could exercise common sense and compassion. Police officers like prosecutors and the courts don't have to be social workers to call one if the situation dictates; nor do they have to be volunteers with an outreach group or Alcoholics Anonymous to get such groups involved. All they have to do is exercise some compassion-based common sense. As Len Saxon, an old friend once put it, all the laws of the land and workings of the criminal justice system are meant to be a wise man's guide, not a fool's Bible.

ACKNOWLEDGEMENTS

Special thanks to all of the Highway of Tears victims' families who accepted and supported my involvement without question. To my friend, Ross Annand for his support and old-school-style advice; author and friend Melia McClure for editing my manuscript, being an empathetic listener, and providing invaluable insight and answers to life's difficult questions; my previous RCMP NCOs (bosses), the late Art Fieldsen, Willie Schmidt and Jim O'Malley, all so dissentingly different, yet all in their own way, committed to a compassionate common-sense approach to ensuring equal justice for everyone; lawyers Norman J. Groot, Melody Martin and the late Michael Ragona QC, for all of their *pro bono* legal advice; my friends Marilyn Fulton, Sharon Hurd, Ken, Rose and Jazlyn Luggie, Diane Nakamura, Gabor and Collette Oliver, Solvig Olsson, and Lisa Wybrow, for their help and support; the Reverend Lloyd Thomas for getting involved; Prince George SAR members Dean Price and Jeff Smedley for literally saving the day; Tony Romeyn for all his work on the original Highway of Tears website which was invaluable to me in my research; Nancy Ray, Jamie Thompson and friends, for their much appreciated fundraising efforts; Matthew Gaster for being brave enough to volunteer to help edit my original first few chapters and get me on track; Cheryl Cohen for her words of wisdom and editing; and my publisher Richard Dionne, for his expertise and time in polishing my manuscript.

And finally, thank you to the hundreds of people from all walks of life who decided to trust me, including members of the RCMP, all of whom went out of their way to help me, sometimes at great risk to their personal safety and careers. I will forever be indebted.

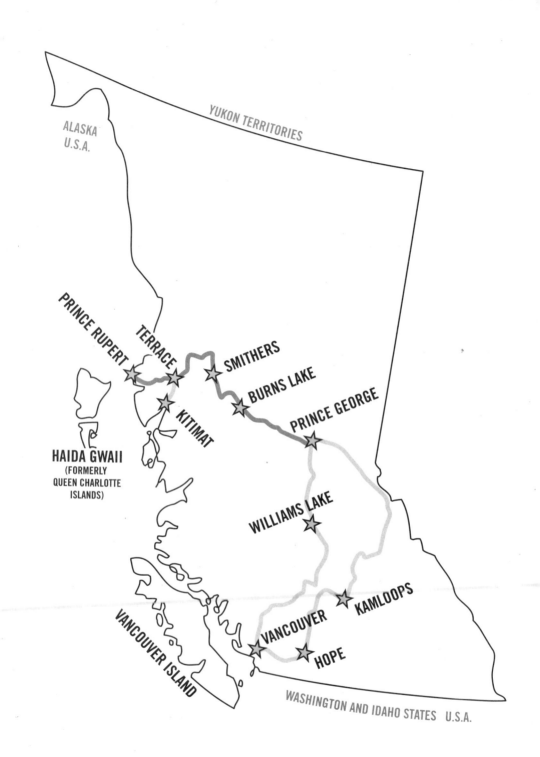

ALASKA
U.S.A.

YUKON TERRITORIES

PRINCE RUPERT

TERRACE

SMITHERS

BURNS LAKE

KITIMAT

PRINCE GEORGE

HAIDA GWAII
(FORMERLY
QUEEN CHARLOTTE
ISLANDS)

WILLIAMS LAKE

VANCOUVER ISLAND

KAMLOOPS

VANCOUVER

HOPE

WASHINGTON AND IDAHO STATES U.S.A.

INTRODUCTION

The 724 kilometre stretch of Highway 16 connecting the cities of Prince George and Prince Rupert on Canada's West Coast is infamously known as the Highway of Tears. It has been speculated that as many as thirty or more women have been murdered or gone missing on this stretch of highway since 1974, and to date, all these cases remain unsolved. This dreadful reality is now so widely known that in his book *Don't Go There*, Peter Greenberg, renowned travel writer and editor for NBC and CBS, dubbed Highway 16 "one of his must-miss places in the world."[6]

I'm a former Mountie who now works as a private investigator, and since December 2005 I have been obsessed with trying to help solve these cases. My inspiration: Helen Betty Osborne, the young Cree woman who, at age nineteen, was abducted and brutally murdered near The Pas, Manitoba in 1971. For some inexplicable reason I had found myself following the RCMP investigation into her death even after I was transferred from Manitoba to British Columbia in 1977. Her case was eventually solved in 1987, sixteen years after her tragic death. Along the way, a Manitoba justice inquiry concluded the following: Helen Betty Osborne's death was fuelled by racism and sexism; she had fallen victim to vicious stereotypes born of ignorance and aggression; while racism marred the initial RCMP investigation. The justice inquiry made over 150 recommendations; however, like so many other reports and recommendations involving Canada's Aboriginal people, most were never acted upon.[7]

Thirty-five years after that murder, two provinces away and 1,800 kilometres west, the RCMP's prevailing attitude toward the Highway of Tears investigation can be likened to that surrounding the Helen Betty Osborne case. Thus, Helen Betty became the inspiration for my Tears investigation.

In 2013, a Human Rights Watch report on *Abusive Policing and Failures in Protection of Indigenous Women and Girls in Northern British Columbia, Canada* noted that the Native Women's Association of Canada (NWAC) had documented 582 cases of murdered and missing women nationally since the 1960s. The NWAC calculated that thirty-nine percent of these cases, or about twenty per year, occurred after 2000, and concluded that if women and girls in the general Canadian population had been murdered or gone missing at the same rate, Canada would have lost 18,000 women and girls since the late 1970s. We now know that the numbers of murdered and missing are much higher than the figure documented in the aforementioned report, because in May 2014, the RCMP acknowledged there were "1,186 police-recorded incidents of Aboriginal homicides and unsolved missing women investigations."[8]

The report outlines the failure of law enforcement to deal effectively with the problem of missing and murdered Indigenous women and girls in Northern British Columbia, where a Human Rights Watch investigation found a lack of oversight, a lack of accountability for police misconduct, and a failure to protect. This inadequacy on the part of the RCMP has resulted in women and girls having little faith in the very police forces responsible for their own protection.

While it can be said that this mistrust represents the residual effects of residential schools, more recent events also contribute greatly to the issue. In 2013, Human Rights Watch researchers documented alleged abuses of women at the hands of the police dating back decades; women not being taken seriously; investigating officers biased against the victims because they were Indigenous women and girls. In one interaction with police an Indigenous leader who was trying to report a fourteen-year-old girl missing from a group home was asked why he was calling and what he expected them to do. Human Rights Watch researchers were told about police officers making a determination about the seriousness of a case depending on whether or not the missing person was a repeat offender, or known to the criminal justice system; and when investigations did occur, victim-blaming by police was not uncommon.[9]

Nevertheless, the RCMP responded by suggesting women could come forward with complaints without fear of retaliation, totally ignoring the fact that Indigenous women have no faith in police or our justice system. In other words, no corrective actions were offered.

Throughout my investigation of the Highway of Tears cases, I've met people whose stories are so personal, intimate and intense that they've often made me cry, laugh, and feel despairing, disgusted and depressed, all at the same time. My Tears journey has also convinced me that similar injustices are occurring across Canada with regards to other murdered and missing women's cases, and it is this belief that has pushed me to bring more public awareness to this incredibly serious problem.

When I began my Tears journey, the RCMP subtly attempted to discourage me by not returning the calls I made when I wanted to provide them with information I had uncovered about the murdered and missing women and girls cases I was investigating, ignoring me as though I didn't exist. When that tactic failed, they tried to discredit me. And when that failed, they threatened me with the possible revocation of my private investigator's licence, eventually threatening me in writing that I could be charged under the *Criminal Code of Canada* if I continued this investigation.

What the RCMP didn't realize was that the more they threatened and attempted to publicly discourage and discredit me, the greater my credibility became among people who lived in the northern communities scattered along the Highway of Tears. Many of these individuals I talked with freely identified themselves as having criminal backgrounds, including drug dealing, prostitution and time done in prison for one crime or another. When I started my investigation they saw me as an outsider, an ex-cop who was still "one of the boys." Not surprisingly, many had experienced ill treatment at the hands of the RCMP. But thanks to the RCMP's negative treatment of me, people along Highway 16 soon started seeing me as part of their community. And that's when they began to help.

Solving the Highway of Tears cases is my obsession. As a result I have spent thousands of hours of my own time on this *pro bono* private investigation, conducting open-source research; interviewing countless potential witnesses; engaging in dialogue with the few RCMP investigators who would talk to me; submitting Freedom of Information requests; consulting with documentary film producers; and being involved in dozens of radio and television interviews. Eventually, I became an unofficial expert on the subject. During my investigative journey into several of the cases along the Highway of Tears, I also uncovered, accumulated and recorded information from a multitude of sources, information that would have otherwise remained undisclosed to the public, barring a highly focused official public inquiry.

The vast amount of information and knowledge that I've gained as a result of this has led to many interviews by local, national and international media. Producers have asked for my assistance and I've also been asked to appear in a number of documentaries, offers that I have declined to date. Unintentionally, I have also become the "go-to guy" for victims and their families, as a source of free information to help them convince police investigators, many of whom have demonstrated an arrogant lack of interest in investigating their cases, to get motivated to do their jobs.

Obstruction of Justice is in large part an account of what has happened since 2005 when I started investigating the Highway of Tears disappearances and murders. It is my personal account about the missing and murdered women in Northern British Columbia, all of whom were Aboriginal but one. It is based on my hundreds of hours of research, dozens of interviews and often unbelievable first-hand experiences. They are all true events.

My story is driven by my personal experiences and hopefully, it will pave the way for readers to make up their own minds about the Highway of Tears tragedies. It's also aimed to raise some important questions. Is there a two-tiered system of police investigation, one for Aboriginal women and another for Canada's general non-Aboriginal population? Did the RCMP attempt to mislead the general public about their investigations? Did the RCMP investigators of the day believe it was possible to solve some of these cases, and if so, why didn't they? What, if anything, did and can government do to resolve the problems? Will I become "roadkill" on this search for truth? Despite all the problems and bungling, I hang on to the hope that all the sadness and feelings of helplessness the victims' families have endured for years will one day be relieved with some sense of closure.

1. THE JOURNEY

"When you know who you are; when your mission is clear and you burn with the inner fire of unbreakable will; no cold can touch your heart; no deluge can dampen your purpose. You know that you are alive."—Duwamish Chief Si'ahl (1780–1866)

My tires chirped as I made a hard left off Central Street into the parking lot at Grandma's Inn. The wheels had barely quit rolling when I jumped out of the car and ran to the door of my motel room. I fumbled with the key, and when the door finally opened, I ran to the bathroom to puke. As much as I wanted to, I couldn't, so I got up off all fours and sat on the bed with my head in my hands. What the hell was I doing?

Had it been even slightly practical, I would have climbed into my car and driven as fast as I could out of Prince George and back to obscurity in Vancouver, never admitting to anyone that I had ever heard about the Highway of Tears. Unfortunately, it was too late for that. I had been investigating the Highway of Tears disappearances for over a year and my publicly planned next step had already brought out reporters from as far away as Calgary to cover the next day's events.

Grandma's is one of the motels I stay at when working in Prince George. The old girl is not fancy, but she is economical, centrally located, very clean, and her kitchen turns out great home-style meals at an affordable price. When I started staying there in 2006, I noticed little red stickers on the dresser mirrors notifying guests that after midnight, no one worked the motel's front desk, so if needed, you could call security at Grandma's sister motel down the block. This was a subtle clue that Prince George was a rough town, something that *Maclean's* magazine confirmed a few years later when it ranked it the most dangerous city in Canada.

I also like Grandma's because you can park your car right outside your motel room door, making it ideal for a light sleeper who wants to keep an eye on his vehicle and any unwanted visitors who might show up unannounced during the night. When I'm suddenly awakened by the sounds of someone prowling around in the dark outside, it's very easy to surreptitiously check on them by slightly moving a corner of the curtain to one side.

As I sat on the bed that day, my stomach churning, my entire body felt stricken with that sick-gut feeling first-time criminals get just after being caught by police or, worse yet, sentenced to a stretch in prison for the first time. I hadn't done anything criminal, but my two meetings that day with Staff Sergeant Quintin Smith, the stocky Mountie in charge of the Prince George General Investigations Section, made me feel that I had.

Whether I had done something wrong was irrelevant, as he so succinctly put it, because if in his opinion I didn't follow his instructions to the letter, he would call the British Columbia Ministry of Justice, Security Programs Division, and have my private investigator's licence revoked. I seriously doubted he had the power to have my licence pulled on his say-so, and I suspect he sensed I had doubts about his ability to make good on his threat. In fact, at one point during our conversation the staff sergeant became so agitated that the pink in his plump cheeks turned fire-engine red, then quickly spread up over his ears, past his forehead, and eventually covered every millimetre of his shaved head. I thought he was going to clamber over his desk and hit me. He didn't, but in the old days before political correctness, and what actor Clint Eastwood once alluded to as "a generation of whiners worrying about the psychological effects of their actions"[1]—a modern tendency which I believe helped change the RCMP forever and not always for the better—things might have been different. Although Smith's behaviour toward me might seem unacceptable and out of place in today's RCMP, he was old school as was I, and I admired that he had the balls to take the stand he did.

My grudging admiration for the guy came of course from the fact I am ex-RCMP. But the fact is, I had actually been a Mountie-in-waiting since age six—yep, way back in 1953. That's when I started school and was seated at a small wooden desk in a row of other small wooden desks set out to accommodate about twenty students, Grades 1 through 12. All of us were to be taught by the only schoolteacher assigned to that school. This was the start of his first teaching job since graduation from teachers' college, a goal he had set for himself after concluding his tour of duty in Europe as a member of the Royal Canadian Engineers in the Second World War. I was proud, not just because this was my first day in Grade 1 and the start of a totally new life experience, but because the man who was standing at the front of the classroom was my dad.

My grade's assignment was a colouring project. I had a Lone Ranger book in front of me, and I was going to be colouring scenes of my hero. I had no idea the Lone Ranger was a fictional character who fought to right injustice. All that mattered was that he was a cowboy, and that's what I was going to be when I grew up.

I soon became consumed by the story on the page. It was as though I was there, right alongside my hero. I watched helplessly as the Lone Ranger slowly rode up to a huge rock. Sensing danger was lurking out of sight, he drew his revolver. And there I saw what he could not—a man on one knee, rifle ready, waiting to ambush my idol. I could hardly breathe; my heart raced. I had to do something. Then, as he rode closer to the rock, two shots rang out.

Unfortunately for me, the shots weren't from the Lone Ranger's gun, nor from his adversary's. From the looks on their faces, my dad and all the other students in that little school had no doubt who had in fact shouted, "Bang! Bang!" The next thing I remember were the tears that rolled down my face as I stood in front of the teacher's desk, my dad's desk, anticipating the sting on my nervous, sweaty little hands that would come from the brown leather strap he was slowly removing from his desk drawer. Not even the Lone Ranger's courage was enough to get me through my Grade 1 experience tear-free. However, by the end of the day I was sure of two things—the Lone Ranger was just a fictional colouring-book character and I needed to choose a new career: I would become a Mountie when I grew up because I would still get to ride a horse, pack a pistol and right injustice.

Ironically, after I had waited my entire young life to be sworn in as a regular member of the RCMP, the Mounties revamped their basic recruit training and I found myself in one of the first new troops *not* being taught how to ride horses. Instead, we had to be content cleaning stables and grooming horses still ridden by the last of our predecessors to complete the original training. I did get to wear a gun belt and carry a gun though, but when I opened the box that held the .38-calibre Smith & Wesson revolver, I discovered, to my surprise and deep disappointment, that it was used, passed down from a former member of the force who had quit, retired, been fired or died. Undeterred, when the force asked for applicants to join the Musical Ride, I immediately applied, only to be told that

I was an unacceptable candidate because, at six foot two, I was too tall. At the time, my height would have disrupted the aesthetics of the era, which required the riders to be roughly the same height as they sat mounted on their horses in their scarlet tunics. According to RCMP legend, the Musical Ride was first performed as early as 1876. Later it was used by members of the North-West Mounted Police to display their riding prowess while providing entertainment for the community. It eventually evolved into the Canadian tradition it is today.[2] That said, I still feel a little bit bad about not making it.

In April 1967, following a nine-month basic recruit training that began in Regina, Saskatchewan and finished in Penhold, Alberta, I was posted to the Dauphin Rural Detachment in Manitoba. Upon arrival, I was required to give the officer in charge of Dauphin Sub-Division a letter requesting I be issued a three-cell flashlight, a storm coat (the Mountie's name for a parka), and twelve rounds of .38-calibre ammunition for my bullet-less revolver. Unfortunately, in keeping with doing things "the RCMP way," my sergeant wouldn't issue me bullets until another sergeant ensured that I was qualified to carry a loaded gun. There was no shooting range in Dauphin so until we went for a drive in the country to shoot squirrels in the bush, I had to walk around town, in uniform, with a gun that had no bullets. *What if, while at work and dressed in uniform, I witnessed a bank robbery or a murder as I walked to lunch?* Such "what ifs" became endless, so to shut me up a senior co-worker lent me six rounds until mine were issued and signed for.

Less than a year later, in January 1968, I received orders that I was being transferred north to Gillam, Manitoba. There was no road into Gillam so the mode there would be an overnight train on the CNR's mixed-freight to Churchill, on Hudson Bay, the last stop before the train's southward return. The day before my departure, the constable I was replacing stopped by the barracks to fill me in on what I could expect in Gillam. He told me that the Kettle River Generating Station construction camp there was policed by fourteen private security guards, and two RCMP members who were also responsible for policing the nearby town and surrounding area. The town itself had a population of just over 300 residents, made up of members of the Fox Creek First Nations, Hydro employees, and various owners and employees of the Kettle River construction camp, located at the end of a six-kilometre gravel road that cut through the muskeg. The camp was home to 2,500 men and 52 women. The latter were mostly in their late teens and early twenties and known as Crawley's Dollies because, although they were officially employed by the Crawley & McCracken Company as camp caterers and housekeepers, some provided additional, unofficial services which were not spoken of.

The men at camp came from all over North America and Europe. Their backgrounds varied. There were regular guys, men escaping ex-wives and custody payments, and hard-core gamblers and criminals. Workers were housed in two-man rooms, in twenty-four bunkhouses, working ten-hour shifts, six days a week, with six days of leave every three months which included paid transportation 1,000 kilometres south to civilization: the city of Winnipeg.[3]

Churchill and Hudson Bay were 250 kilometres north by rail, and it seemed to me that the only people going there were tourists hoping to get some pictures of a polar bear. To compensate for the isolation and lack of social activity, there was a "girls' quarters," complete with a sitting room and stereo record player, and here male visitors were entertained from seven to eleven in the evening. The site also had a theatre, dining room, chapel and, more in keeping with the men working there, a recreation hall, which was the first of its kind in the province where men were allowed to gamble their cheques away. This hall was open twenty-four hours a day. After the only drinking establishment in town curiously burned to the ground, its owners were even more curiously allowed to build an on-site, 320-person beverage room, described as the centre of *free-time activity*.

I boarded the train to Gillam with all my worldly possessions padlocked in the blue metal wardrobe trunk I bought while in training. The train ride took about thirty hours and, half an hour before our arrival at midnight the following day, train conductor Jim Ritchie, who had introduced himself the day before, asked me to follow him to the baggage car where I would disembark. Before my trip, I had been issued a CNR freight train permit allowing me to travel in the caboose for free while on police business. I soon found out that Jim never used the caboose because he was usually too busy maintaining law and order. I never spent much time in the caboose either because whenever Jim invited me to ride with him, I usually came aboard in uniform, and my presence helped with the law-and-order part of his job. In those days, part of this role involved rounding up all the drunks and troublemakers and herding them into the last passenger car. Once there, he locked the doors at each end, turned the heat up as high as it would go, and checked on those passengers regularly until they all passed out, waking them only to boot them off the train at their final destination. When I think of Canadian train travel today, the Rocky Mountaineer comes to mind with its glass-domed coaches, gourmet food and breathtaking scenery. In my youth, the CNR train north was more about fistfights and drunken, violently sick passengers puking wherever they happened to find themselves at the time.

Gillam's subarctic climate was in full swing that January night, with the temperature well into the minus-twenties Celsius. The night frost fog that often engulfed the town had also engulfed the train station, including the entire train, which was only slightly visible thanks to the amber fog lights that burned along the station platform.

It was like Halloween in January. As the door slowly creaked open I saw the detachment's paddy wagon backed up toward the train with its rear doors open. Corporal Willie Schmidt, my new boss, stood waiting. The giant of a man was a Manitoba legend, sent to rough communities to make them safe for those of us who followed. He stood there in his personally customized police uniform, one I never saw before or since. His open jacket was not the standard RCMP storm coat with RCMP patch on the shoulders. Instead it was the beaded parka worn by most civilian northerners. The flaps of his issue fur hat were lowered to protect his ears from the cold, and his leather gloves were topped with three-inch cuffs decorated with colourful Aboriginal beadwork. Willie was wearing his issue "long blues" (yellow-striped pants) without a gun belt, because as I later learned, he never carried a gun while working. His footwear consisted of mukluks, an authentic type of leather Aboriginal footwear.

As I slid my trunk to the edge of the boxcar door, the gravity of my transfer to Gillam, which to me seemed like the end of the world, was slowly sinking in. Before I had a chance to introduce myself, Willie was hauling my trunk out of the baggage car with hands too big to fit in the trunk's handles. I quickly introduced myself, saying I would jump down to help lift it into the wagon. But before I could get on the ground, "Big Willie" had lifted it into the vehicle and was closing the back doors.

I never really grasped how Willie Schmidt went about making things safer for guys like me until rumours started circulating in town about his pending transfer. I first heard it like this. I was in the process of arresting a construction worker in camp for some minor offence. As I opened the back door of the police car so he could get in, he hesitated for a second, smiled and said: "I'll get in your cop car this time, but just wait until Big Willie's gone!"

In those days RCMP detachments like Gillam were notorious for having usually more than one tough guy wanting to make a name for himself by intimidating and/or beating the crap out of a cop. While I could probably recover from any injuries I might receive, the thought of the public humiliation to follow forced me to become pretty damn tough myself. That's my excuse for becoming pretty good at the now-outdated draconian skill of street fighting.

Police recruits were taught a combination of various martial arts such as judo, karate and jiu-jitsu for self-defence—or street fighting. The emphasis was placed on winning. (I still have my 1965 edition of Ottawa police officer George Sylvain's book, *Scientific Method of Police Fighting*.) As much as that helped, these skills were never foolproof. My skinny beanpole body still suffered the bruises, aches and pains that followed unscheduled bouts of fighting that sprang up while trying to arrest one or another of the camp's concrete-and-steel workers.

Not everything was fists and fury, though. There were other matters of a more domestic nature. Only half a dozen single women resided in town among the large number of lonely and unhappily married women whose husbands worked too many hours, drank too much, paid too little attention or were physically and mentally abusive. Sometimes the wives turned to other men for comfort, started drinking heavily themselves, or a few of the lucky ones finally got so fed up that they packed their bags and headed south on the train, never to be seen or heard from again. It was difficult for women to escape, but virtually impossible if you were an Aboriginal woman, most of whom were unemployed. The few who had jobs still, had few if any places to turn for support.

My friend Maureen was pals with one such young married woman who was looking for a way to escape her abusive marriage. In an effort to help, Maureen decided to go out of her way to hook us up. There was a problem with this plan for me because the woman was married, and I was also married, at least in my mind, to the RCMP. To make matters worse, I knew that despite the fact that the force was notorious for extramarital affairs (and senior members of management were equally notorious for turning a blind eye to it), there was no tolerance for a member who got involved in any sort of romantic affair with a Native woman, let alone a married woman who was well connected to her Aboriginal community.

Moral issues aside, it was a no-brainer, even for a rookie like me: getting involved romantically would have been a career breaker.

In April 1969 I was eventually transferred south—not to the sleepy Manitoba farming community I had been dreaming about, but 300 kilometres away to Thompson, to a city police force. In my mind this was not a transfer to an RCMP detachment. Had I wanted to join the city police, I would have signed up with a real city police organization like the one in Saskatoon or Regina in my home province. I didn't like the transfer and apparently, my soon-to-be fourth detachment commander got wind of this long before I arrived, and he seemed to take it personally.

In hindsight, I should have tried to stay out of his way and walked on eggshells like many others in the detachment, but that would have been out of character for me. So I began a silent but obvious protest. When he assigned me steady afternoon and nightshifts without the dayshifts my peers enjoyed, I retaliated by doing little things for the sole purpose of pissing him off. In the mornings he was like a wounded bear so when he telephoned the office for a police car to pick him up, it seemed like each and everyone on shift went out of their way to make sure they were busy doing something else. Not me. I would hang around his neighbourhood to be the first to pick him up. Once he opened the door I would greet him with a very cheery (and loud), "Good morning, Staff!" I sensed from the lack of verbal response that this drove him crazy.

In September 1969 I was called into his office and shown a very poor performance review that he completed about me. He also explained how fair it was of him to give me an opportunity to resign honourably before he fired me. I didn't resign. And wasn't fired. Instead I foolishly upped my childish game-playing, aggravating him even more at every opportunity.

Months later and still on the job during a short-handed Saturday-afternoon shift, I became the arresting officer and lead investigator in a complaint that five young Caucasian males had raped a thirteen-year-old Aboriginal girl in the basement of a house where she had been babysitting. I headed to the crime scene and was within ten blocks of it when I spotted five young men walking away from the general direction of the house. I pulled over, got out of the car and asked them, point-blank, if they had just come from the house in question. All five denied it. Because I had not yet interviewed the alleged victim, I had no way of knowing if in fact a rape had taken place. And if a rape had indeed occurred, I had no description of the suspects. Just as I was about to get back in the police car and continue to the crime scene, my gut feeling, an intuitive ability I had always relied on in the past, told me these men were responsible for the crime. I couldn't just drive away and leave them standing there, but if I was wrong, it would be a quick, disgraceful end to my career. I opened the back door of the police car and heard myself telling the men I didn't believe them, that they were all under arrest and needed to get in the car. One by one, in silence, they looked into the back seat of the car, then at me and then finally at one another. It was as though they were all waiting for the other one to make a decision that they, as a group, could agree with and act on. If just one defied my orders and refused to get in the car, all five would defy my orders. The odds weren't in my favour. "Get in the car!" I growled. Then one of them slowly, reluctantly, got into the car. Like sheep, the other four slowly followed until they were all sitting in the cage in the back seat. I slammed the door shut.

My boss denied my request for members of our detachment's plainclothes unit to take over the investigation. I can only speculate he was setting me up for what he thought was going to be my investigative failure, leaving him an opportunity to get rid of me forever. But it wasn't to be. With the help of two friends, Constable Ken Schmidt and senior Mountie Jerry Anderson, and the hard work of legendary Crown counsel Orsten Wright and his protégé Charles Newcomb, the five accused men were charged with rape and eventually convicted. Their case is now part of the case law found in the *Criminal Code of Canada* as precedence used to determine a victim's age. My staff sergeant reckoned I must have "found myself."

Eventually, I got my wish and was transferred to a sleepy farming community 800 kilometres south. However, a short time later, my old boss got his wish: his behaviour drastically soured my opinion of the force, so I resigned.

Four years later, the RCMP was fast-tracking ex-members' re-applications to join the force, so I reapplied. Before I was accepted, a federal Veterans Affairs doctor conducted my medical exam. When he learned I was not a new recruit but rather an ex-member who was rejoining the force, he looked at me and shook his head. As I jumped up and down in the nude on one foot, my balls bouncing in the wind in front of his open ground-floor window, the VA doctor quietly made an observation: "You should be down the hall instead, being examined by a fucking psychiatrist."

The VA doctor was probably right, but I missed the camaraderie or, as the RCMP would say, the *esprit de corps*. I also missed the action, the opportunity to fight crime, and more importantly, the opportunity to help people. Once back in the force I realized that not only had I changed, but the force had changed too, but not necessarily for the good. It had become more political. Perception was often more important than reality. I didn't fit in so I resigned for the second time.

———

Three decades later, now a successful private investigator and at the urging of my wife (and the inspiration I gained from the Helen Betty Osborne case), I decided to see if I could help do something about the missing and murdered women's cases along the Highway of Tears.

When I first began visiting towns and cities along Highway 16, I made a point of stopping by the RCMP detachments that policed them. It had been a while since I was last in a northern RCMP office. My goal this time was to introduce myself and attempt to establish some kind of rapport with one or two of the cops along the way. However, I was rarely able to establish rapport with anyone from the RCMP. When I introduced myself to a member at the Burns Lake Detachment office, for instance, he wouldn't even come out from behind the bulletproof glass partition to shake my hand. So I tried to hand him a business card through the slot in the glass. He instinctively reached out to take it, but quickly pulled back before touching my card as though he feared just being in possession of it might adversely affect his career. Another time in Smithers I introduced myself to a young cop at the front desk. When I asked to speak to the staff sergeant in charge, the constable quickly stressed, "He's gonna want to talk to you!" I got the impression the staff sergeant had been saying quite a bit about me, but none of it was very favourable. Unfortunately, he had gone out for coffee only minutes earlier. When a police radio call went out asking the boss to return to the office, we learned to our surprise that the coffee was more important. I gave my business card to the disillusioned constable and explained I was going to be working in town for a few days and I would happily return to talk to his boss if he called. He never did.

A few years later, I found myself visiting Smithers Detachment again, this time with a man who claimed to be a witness to Ramona Wilson's murder. The witness told me he was the second person who tried giving the Smithers cops this information. The first person, a now-deceased woman he knew, had been laughed at by police and told to go home. The young RCMP constable didn't laugh at us, but he did ask me who Ramona Wilson was, despite the fact that she was born, raised and murdered in the area. An eavesdropping civilian employee interrupted our conversation, asking if I had an appointment. An appointment? I was standing in a police office with a potential witness to a murder and she was suggesting I go away and make an appointment. I couldn't believe it.

Unfortunately, as I was about to find out, these types of reactions often seemed to be the norm during my ten-year investigation on the Highway of Tears.

2. THE HIGHWAY

*"The odds of being chosen as a serial killer's victim are extraordinarily slim.
It's kind of like a lottery winner, only in reverse."*[1]
— Rob Gordon, Director of Simon Fraser University's School of Criminology

No one in Northern British Columbia seems to know the exact origin of the phrase "Highway of Tears," now used to describe the 724-kilometre stretch of Highway 16, a deadly road that starts in coastal Prince Rupert then winds through the scenic wilderness of the Coast Mountains to connect to inland Prince George.

Perhaps the name was borrowed and slightly revised from the "Trail of Tears," when in the 1830s Cherokee families were removed from their homes in the American South and forced to travel hundreds of miles north through Georgia to Oklahoma, resulting in many deaths and other untold tragedies. Perhaps the name originated in the late nineteenth century, when Aboriginal women were loaded with packs and forced by men in their community to walk across a 100-foot-high handmade bridge above Bulkley River Canyon in British Columbia to test its repair.[2, 3] Or maybe the name originated later in the early twentieth century with the opening of the Lejac Indian Residential School on Highway 16, notorious for being a place where children were brought and suffered many abuses at the hands of their custodians.[4]

What we do know is that the Highway of Tears is a section of the Yellowhead Highway named after fur trader and explorer Pierre Bostonais whose streaked hair resulted in the nickname *Tête Jaune*, or Yellowhead in English. There is little or no habitation along this highway, with the exception of the few communities it passes through, nine of which recently had an average crime rate per capita more than two times that of seventeen municipalities in Metro Vancouver.[6] At the end of the Highway of Tears, east of Prince George, the Yellowhead or Highway 16 continues on to connect British Columbia with Alberta, Saskatchewan and Manitoba.

According to John Douglas, a former Chief of the FBI's Elite Serial Crime Unit and author of *Mindhunter*, "A very conservative estimate is that there are between thirty-five to fifty active serial killers in the United States at any given time."[7] There are no Canadian statistics or concrete speculations as to the number of serial killers at work in British Columbia that I am aware of, but because of its coastal access, climate, scenery and economic significance, the province not only attracts tourists and immigrants from all over the world, but also human traffickers, drug dealers and our own bizarre brand of serial killers.

One such BC killer is the late Clifford Robert Olson. Olson was convicted in 1982 of murdering eleven people, three boys and eight girls, all between the ages of nine and eighteen. The legal case became exceedingly controversial when it was later revealed that the RCMP offered him "cash for bodies," an arrangement where he got paid to tell authorities where the victims were buried. The bodies, discovered over a nine-month period, had been scattered in isolated areas within a ninety-kilometre radius of Vancouver. All the while Olson was free from prison on mandatory supervision. The victims had all been drugged and then subjected to horrendous physical crimes before being killed.[8] Olson later bragged that the deal was "a freebie." At his insistence, his wife eventually received the dividends: a $100,000 "cash for bodies" trust fund, the validity of which was unsuccessfully challenged in the Supreme Court of British Columbia by families of seven of the victims.[9]

British Columbia is also home to the more recently convicted (2007) Robert "Willie" Pickton. Willie operated a pig farm in Port Coquitlam. Although Pickton confessed to a mind-boggling forty-nine murders, he was charged with killing twenty-six women and convicted for killing six.[10] The police investigation is estimated to have cost over $100 million, the largest part of which represented the RCMP investigation, which carried a price tag of some $70 million.[11] Although there has been no evidence presented to the public that Willie Pickton had anything to do with any of the Highway of Tears cases, it is somewhat curious that his mother and father once owned four parcels of land in the Peace River region.[12]

This area includes the town of Hudson's Hope north of Highway 16, and location of one murder victim being investigated by the RCMP. (Something the public wasn't told: in 2002, as the result of a lawsuit filed against the RCMP with regards to their involvement in the Pickton investigation, an RCMP external review was conducted called "Project: EVEN-HANDED." Among other things it noted: "This does not preclude the fact that several other high-profile suspects including Pickton are operating as serial killers in the Province of British Columbia."[13])

Other notorious BC offenders include Cody Alan Legebokoff who in November 2010, was arrested and eventually charged with the murder of a fifteen-year-old Fraser Lake girl and three other women. In mid-September 2014, the BC Supreme Court in Prince George sentenced Legebokoff on four counts of first-degree murder. He received life in prison with no parole for twenty-five years.

The area is not without its disturbingly bizarre either. Take Kayla Bourque, a former Simon Fraser University student originally from Prince George. In 2013 the twenty-three-year-old pleaded guilty to "causing unnecessary pain and suffering to an animal, killing or injuring an animal, and possessing a weapon for a dangerous purpose." In fact the media reported that she had been described as a "serial killer in waiting."[14] The five-foot-four, 130-pound woman with black hair and brown eyes was arrested after telling a fellow student

she had dismembered cats in her hometown of Prince George, a[...]
that she fantasized about murdering someone. After her arrest, a bag
containing a knife, razor blade, syringe, mask, garbage bags and zap
straps was found in her dorm room, together with a video of her
torturing her cat and eviscerating her family's dog.[15] Although she
was considered high risk to reoffend, in early 2016 a judge ordered
she be allowed unescorted day trips in the community.

While violent crime links British Columbia's most notorious
criminals, other than being located along Highway 16, the cities
and communities involved in the Highway of Tears investigations
have little in common. The city of Prince George, for instance,
was established in 1807 and named in honour of King George III.
Although Prince George's population is approximately nine times
less than the City of Vancouver, its crime rate is almost two times
higher—and so is the caseload per police officer.[16] "PG," as it is
called by locals, is the easternmost community on the Highway of
Tears and the largest city in Northern British Columbia; it has a
number of historic sites as well, including shopping centres and
offers its residents theatrical and musical events, fine dining—all
rare in the north—and instant access to outdoor activities such as
hiking, skiing, fishing, golfing and camping.

From an investigator's point of view however—and with a
serial-killer theory in mind -- it is notable that Prince George is

ographically unique within the province because it serves as both a north-south and east-west transportation hub. The city is dissected north and south by Highway 97, which runs north to the Northwest Territories, Yukon and Alaska, where by September 2000, six women had been murdered in Anchorage. Their cases remain unsolved.[17] Highway 97 also runs south to Vancouver and the United States where, as previously mentioned, there are a fair share of serial killers. Prince George is also dissected east-west by Highway 16 which connects the port of Prince Rupert to Alberta and the rest of Canada.

When I first heard of Prince George in the mid-sixties, forestry dominated the local economy, misuse of alcohol coloured the crime scene, and it was not uncommon for RCMP members to suffer humiliation and physical abuse at the hands of Paul Bunyan-sized loggers. It was the place where the biggest, burliest and toughest rookies just out of RCMP training were sent; their size and strength were quickly put to the test as they literally *fought* crime. Today, the forest industry is faltering due to the mountain pine beetle, which has killed 726-million cubic metres of timber and is affecting an estimated 17.5-million hectares more.[18]

Now drugs and gangs fuel the local crime scene. In 2010 and 2011 *Maclean's* magazine ranked Prince George the most dangerous city in Canada, a label that many family-oriented, law-abiding citizens bristle at. In fact, I was recently at a restaurant in downtown Prince George very early one morning where I asked a young RCMP constable if this was "a quiet time" for police. He laughed and told me there was no quiet time because, as he put it, "These people are all crazy!"

Farther west along Highway 16 is Vanderhoof, which was originally founded in 1918 as an artists' retreat. However, farmers attracted by the fertile lands settled there instead, making the town's name, which means "of the farm" in Dutch, rather fitting.[19] Vanderhoof has nineteen churches, many arts-and-crafts businesses, a number of daycare facilities, and food banks. There are slightly more than 3,800 residents with an additional 3,900 populating the surrounding area.[20] In 2014 the Vanderhoof area's crime rate was about 1.6 times higher than that of Vancouver.[21] (There have also been some rather unusual occurrences and activities reported there such as crop circles[22] and a 1995 buffalo mutilation.[23]) The town is also close to the now-demolished Lejac Residential School, which was opened in 1922 and operated by the Roman Catholic Church. Despite the fact that the children there could not speak English, they were still not allowed to speak their native tongue. Four of the more infamous cases at Lejac involved Allen Willie, Andrew Paul, Maurice Justin and Johnny Michael. The boys ran away on New Year's Day in 1937; it was thirty degrees below zero at the time. One of the boys was dressed in summer clothing, had no hat and was wearing only one rubber boot. All four were found frozen to death on a lake.[24] Although the school has been demolished, a Canada-wide arrest warrant has been issued for Edward Gerald Fitzgerald, a dormitory supervisor who is now living in Ireland. The seventy-something-year-old is charged with ten counts of indecent assault, three counts of gross indecency, two counts of buggery and six counts of common assault.[25]

Vanderhoof was also home to Madison Scott, a twenty-year-old white woman who in 2011 went missing from a party in the Hogsback Lake area, about twenty-four kilometres southeast of the village. Although she has not been named as a Tears victim by police, Madison Scott's case also remains unsolved.

Next on the trip west along Highway 16 and three hours west of Prince George is the Village of Burns Lake. Incorporated in 1913, it has a population of slightly less than 3,000[26] though it serves the surrounding area of Bulkley-Nechako which has more than triple that. Two of the six local First Nations communities are located within Burns Lake's municipal boundaries.[27] There are also three First Nations reserves which are part of the town and another three nearby, making it one of the few communities in the province with an almost equal population of Natives and non-Native Canadians.[28] In 2014 the Burns Lake area had an average crime rate 1.6 times higher than that of Metro Vancouver,[29] and one of the Tears victims' bodies was dumped just east of the village along Highway 16.

Located in the Bulkley Valley between Hudson Bay Mountain to the west and Babine Mountains to the east, sits the town of Smithers with a population of slightly over 5,000.[30] Smithers was created by the Grand Trunk Pacific Railroad in 1913. In 2014 Smithers had an average crime rate 4.9 times higher than that of Vancouver.[31]

Smithers is famous on several accounts. In 1912 one of its former residents, and founder of the Smithers *Interior News*, a man named Joseph Coyle, settled a dispute between a clumsy egg farmer and angry hotel owner by inventing the first egg-safety carton, the forerunner to what is found in supermarkets today.[32] Over time, this remote town has also been the childhood home to half a dozen NHL players. And if the rumour is correct, former late-night talk-show host David Letterman bought a fishing licence near here back in 2005.[33] Sadly, Smithers was home to two Tears victims.

Farther west along Highway 16 is the City of Terrace with a population of some 11,000. In 2014 Terrace had an average crime rate almost 2.5 times higher than Vancouver's.[34] It is the last densely populated city before reaching British Columbia's West Coast. Though located in the Coast Mountains' Skeena Valley, it is only sixty metres above sea level. The Tsimshian First Nations were the first people to occupy the area, and that was more than 10,000 years ago. Today, seven First Nations groups live within close proximity to the city.[35] During the Second World War the city was also scene to the "Terrace Mutiny," the most serious military violation in Canadian history. It began in 1944 when soldiers stationed there heard rumours that they were to be deployed overseas.[36] More recently Terrace has become known as the home of the mystical Kermode bear—or spirit bear—one of the mascots of the 2010 Vancouver Winter Olympics and a prominent First Nations symbol. According to Kitasoo legend, Raven, known as the Creator, "went among the bears and turned every tenth bear white to serve as a reminder of a time when the Earth's great glaciers covered the landscape. That way he could remember the world as it was." Then Raven issued a decree: "The white bears would live here forever in peace."[37] Terrace is home to two Tears victims.

With a population of 15,000,[38] Prince Rupert is found 140 kilometres west of Terrace. In 2014 Prince Rupert had an average crime rate almost 1.5 times higher than Metro Vancouver's.[39] Prince Rupert is the most westerly city along the Highway of Tears and named after Prince Rupert of the Rhine, the first governor of the Hudson's Bay Company. "Rupert," as northerner's call it, is situated on Kaien Island on the rugged BC coastline. Once known as the "Halibut Capital of the World," this city is surrounded by lush old-growth rainforest and has been home to First Nations peoples for thousands of years, as evidenced by petroglyphs and ancient First Nations villages.[40] Rupert is also just 100 kilometres from Haida Gwaii, formerly known as the Queen Charlotte Islands. This ecologically diverse habitat is made up of almost 2,000 islands in the archipelago. Now Rupert is home to a new super-port which, when fully constructed, will be the second largest on North America's West Coast. Prince Rupert was a temporary home to one Tears victim and the last place another was seen before her disappearance.

No matter how many times you make the drive on this desolate mountain highway, through its profoundly beautiful countryside and snow-capped mountains, you can't help being struck with a sense of despair knowing you are alone and vulnerable in the middle of pretty much nowhere. The despair and vulnerability are heightened even more when you realize there is no cellphone service and no gas stations or pay phones between these towns, with the exception of the few sparsely inhabited areas you drive through. The vehicles you pass, including the many trucks, are driven by nameless faces, invisible and haunting if you happen to be making the trip alone at night—or worse, if you're walking along the road or hitchhiking.

3. LOST SOULS

"Being unwanted, unloved, uncared for, forgotten by everybody, I think that is a much greater hunger, a much greater poverty than the person who has nothing to eat."—Mother Teresa

The First Nations people who live along the Highway of Tears are sure of two things: a large number of women and girls have been murdered and gone missing over the past four decades, and all their cases remain unsolved. This despite the existence of the RCMP Project E-PANA, a taskforce created in 2005 following the "E" Division Criminal Operations review and investigation of a series of unsolved murders with links to Highway 16. E-PANA's goal was to determine if a serial killer—or killers—were travelling along major British Columbian highways and murdering women.

Whether a serial killer, or killers are involved remains to be seen, but one thing is certain: no one in these communities believes the missing women are runaways. That said, the police's ability to solve these cases seems to be contingent on resources, or lack thereof. Constable Mike Herchuk, Prince George RCMP media liaison, said they just didn't have the manpower or money to take the extra steps necessary to solve the cases. He said the workload was "pulling officers in a multitude of directions," and "the RCMP have too many unsolved homicides and too many missing persons."

Herchuk added that solving even one of the Highway of Tears cases would call for a celebration. Sergeant Anders Udsen, the man in charge of Smithers' plainclothes investigators, said "that although they were doing what they could when they had the opportunity, officers were burning out because they were working more overtime than they could possibly handle and they just weren't in a position to provide what was needed to get the job done."[1]

It was clear then that more had to be done. So in March 2006, a two-day Highway of Tears Symposium was held in Prince George, organized by the Union of British Columbia Indian Chiefs whose goal was to give their people in BC a global voice.[2] The symposium included families of the victims, RCMP officials, BC's solicitor-general, social workers and First Nations leaders.[3]

By this time, my initial research and investigation had revealed that many people considered fifteen-year-old Monica Ignas to be the first-known Highway of Tears victim. Accordingly, she was the first on my chronological list of victims. Monica disappeared from Terrace on Friday, December 13, 1974. After stopping at a new indoor pool for a swim she set out toward the Old Skeena Bridge and her home in Thornhill, on the other side of the Skeena River. Terrace is the first city just east of Prince Rupert on Highway 16. The day Monica Ignas went missing the temperature averaged a chilly minus one degree Celsius. It surely must have felt much colder having just gone for a swim—a factor that may have led her to accept a ride home from someone. Whatever the case, her strangled body was found, partially nude, in a gravel pit about six kilometres from Terrace on April 6, 1975.

On Thursday, June 13, 1990—about sixteen years after Monica went missing—fifteen-year-old Delphine Nikal, the second Tears victim and the first of two victims from Smithers, telephoned her family to tell them she would be hitchhiking from Smithers to her home in the Village of Telkwa, about fifteen kilometres southeast of town.[4] Delphine's sister Lucy was certain Delphine had been kidnapped by someone she knew because "she wouldn't get into a car with a creepy-looking guy; she'd tell him to get lost and keep walking."[5]

Four years later on Saturday, June 11, 1994, sixteen-year-old Ramona Wilson, the third Tears victim, was last seen hitchhiking east on Highway 16 just outside Smithers. It is believed she was headed to Moricetown. Almost a year later, in April 1995, her body was found in the bush near the Smithers airport. Ramona's mother said she thought the police were doing their best, but "she was not relying on them to deliver justice to her daughter's killer."[6] She complained it took the brutal murder of Melanie Carpenter, a woman from the Lower Mainland, to put the case into perspective for people up in the north. Melanie was a twenty-three-year-old woman that was abducted from her work at a tanning salon in

Surrey in 1995 and murdered. Before he was arrested and questioned, the primary suspect, Fernand Auger, out of jail on parole for armed robbery, committed suicide.[7] Money was raised in Melanie's name, $160,000 was spent on rallies, and 900 telephone lines were opened. For just $2 a minute, callers could listen to a message and contribute to the fight for tougher laws against dangerous offenders.[8] Terrace's Deputy Mayor, Jim Davidson, said Melanie's case touched the entire province. On the other hand, Dianna Ford, the family support coordinator at the Dze L K'ant Friendship Centre in Smithers, said the general reaction to Ramona's case was instead, "Oh, it's just another Native girl who's run away south to live on the streets."[9]

On Friday, July 1, 1994, fifteen-year-old Roxanne Thiara, the fourth Tears victim, was last seen in Prince George before she disappeared. On August 17 her skeletal remains were found in a wooded area near Burns Lake. Roxanne, the daughter of a Cree-Carrier woman, was born in Winnipeg and taken in by her Quesnel, BC stepmother when she was three months old.[10] She was once an honours student but later quit school and became involved in drugs and prostitution. Roxanne's brother-in-law said she was like a daughter to him, but got led astray by other young girls. Burns Lake's Constable Alex Clarke said: "The types of people she hung out with don't want to help with the investigation."[11] That said, about twenty-five people, including street kids in their early teens, attended what was called a "Farewell Evening for Our Friend Roxanne,"[12] organized in August 1994 with the help of BC Ministry of Social Services' *Reconnect*, a program for street kids in Prince George.

Six months passed. Then on Friday, December 6, 1994, the fifth tears victim, Leah Germaine—also known as Leah Cunningham— left a dinner for street kids held at the Native Indian Friendship Centre. She was last seen between 9:00 and 10:00 p.m.[13, 14] Leah was found murdered in the Leslie Road school-yard, a short distance from Highway 16 in southwest Prince George. She had not been sexually assaulted and died from multiple stab wounds. According to an unnamed street worker, Leah got hooked on cocaine and heroin after leaving a turbulent home at age twelve. She was trying to leave behind a life of drug abuse and prostitution when she disappeared.[15]

Tragedy struck again almost a year later. On Saturday, October 7, 1995, sixteen-year-old Lana Derrick, the sixth Tears victim, disappeared. Lana was a forestry student at a college in Houston, BC, where she lived while going to school. She had returned to her parent's home in Thornhill for the Thanksgiving weekend. It's believed she was planning to stay with friends in Terrace before going to her parents' home for Thanksgiving. But she changed her mind, leaving her friend's home at approximately 3:30 a.m. She was never seen again.[16]

Almost three years later, on Friday, August 28, 1998, Alberta

Williams, the seventh Tears victim, was last seen after a party in Bogey's Cabaret, Prince Rupert. She was there with her sister, Claudia, and a few friends to celebrate their last day in town before heading home to Vancouver. They had spent the summer that year working at a local fish plant. Five days later, on September 2, her body was found by hikers near the Tyee Overpass on Highway 16, approximately thirty-seven kilometres east of Prince Rupert. It was confirmed she had been murdered.

At this time, few people in southern British Columbia had ever heard of the Highway of Tears. That changed on Friday, June 21, 2002, when Nicole Hoar, the eighth and only white Tears victim, was last seen hitchhiking at a gas station in Prince George. She was trying to make her way to Smithers to visit her sister. Nicole's disappearance was followed by the first and only high-profile police investigation into the Tears cases which left not only First Nations people along Highway 16 whispering about racial priorities when it comes to the RCMP.

A little over three years later, on Wednesday, September 21, 2005, the ninth Tears victim, Tamara Chipman, was last seen in Prince Rupert. It is believed she had been hitchhiking near Prince Rupert's industrial area in an attempt to get back home to Terrace.

On February 2, 2006 the body of fourteen-year-old murder victim Aielah Saric-Auger was found dumped along Highway 16, east of Prince George. Although her body was found east of Prince

George, outside the Highway of Tears region, I think it important to acknowledge this case here as well.

The list of murdered and missing would grow following the 2006 Highway of Tears Symposium. This conference was held to raise public awareness and create a call for action regarding known cases to date. After the release of its recommendation report, the RCMP were forced to scramble to not only justify why it had no success in closing any of the investigations, but to lay out a forward-thinking plan to resolve the investigative failures.

Some fifteen months later, after having received very little notice, families of the murdered and missing women made their way to Prince George to meet with the RCMP. There had been rumours in the north about a possible break in one of the cases and everyone was praying for a positive announcement. After the meeting one family member told me of the surprise and disappointment: families were bluntly told upon arrival that contrary to rumours, there was no break in any of the cases; instead, the RCMP had called the meeting so victims' families would be first to know that the Highway of Tears investigation in Northern British Columbia was being expanded to include *eighteen* women who had been murdered or gone missing since 1969. The investigation would therefore include unsolved cases along other major highways as well, in BC north to Hudson's Hope and southeast to Kamloops,

Merritt, 100 Mile House and out of province to Hinton, Alberta. This announcement was devastating to the families because it meant less and less time would be spent on their loved one's cases now that the investigation had doubled in size.

The additional nine victims were added to the official list of missing and murdered women's cases in October 2007. They are:·Gloria Moody, who was murdered in Williams Lake in 1969; Micheline Pare, who was murdered in Hudson's Hope in 1970; Gale Weys, who was murdered in Clearwater in 1973; Pamela Darlington, who was murdered in Kamloops in 1973; Colleen MacMillen, who was murdered in 100 Mile House in 1974; Monica Jack, who was murdered in Merritt in 1978; Maureen Mosie, who was murdered in Kamloops in 1981; Shelly-Ann Bascu, who went missing from Hinton, Alberta in 1983; and Aielah Saric-Auger, noted earlier, who was murdered in Prince George in 2006. The list still does not include Monica Ignas.

Why the RCMP added Gloria Moody's name is unclear because in 1998, the Williams Lake *Tribune* reported that her body was found by hunters approximately twelve kilometres outside Williams Lake; Constable John Pilczek, of the Williams Lake RCMP, said the then-thirty-year-old crime was solved, and the file closed as the three local men who were responsible for the murder had since died.[17] Pilczek's brief account of events surrounding Gloria Moody's death was reiterated during the November 19, 2007 morning sitting of BC's Legislative Assembly. Dennis MacKay, a Member of Parliament and former RCMP member, told the Assembly that while in the employ of the RCMP he had been involved in the investigation of Gloria Moody's murder and, more than a decade later, "we got a deathbed confession from two people who had been involved in her homicide."[18]

In 2007, when the *Tribune* asked for clarification regarding Constable Pilczek's 1998 remarks, now-deceased RCMP "E" Division spokesperson, Sergeant Pierre Lemaitre, disagreed about the Moody case, suggesting it's not uncommon for rumours to surface in serious cases, concluding, "if her case had been solved it would not appear on the list."[19]

While the RCMP added nine names, they ignored eight other victims. These were posted on the City of Quesnel website three years later in 2010.[20] Quesnel is a small city of about 25,000 people located on Highway 97, approximately halfway between Prince George and Williams Lake. The names of these eight murdered and missing women are: 1987 murder victim Mary Jane Jimmie; 1972 missing-person Mary Agnes Thomas; 1972 murder victim Laurie Joseph Blanchard; 1978 missing-person Santokh Kaur Johal; 1979 missing-person Janice Ellisabeth Hackh; 1999 murder victim Deena Lyn Braem, whose father Jim was quoted as saying, "if he could give the RCMP a grade it would be a failing grade;"[21] 2004 missing-person Barbara Anne Lanes; and 2006 missing-person Julie Oakley Parker.

Another four names that didn't make the RCMP E-PANA list of victims are those of the Jack family. The last time anyone heard from Ronald Jack, his wife Doreen, their nine-year-old son Russell and four-year-old son Ryan before they disappeared forever was when Ronald telephoned his mother from a payphone at 1:30 a.m. on August 2, 1989. Calling from Bedneski Resort on Highway 16, about fifty kilometres west of Prince George, he told his mother that he and his family would be gone for ten days to two weeks. *The Highway of Tears Symposium Recommendation Report* speculated that "a predator, knowing this family was impoverished, used the offer of employment at either a ranch or logging camp as a lure."[22] More than a quarter-century later, their cases remain unsolved, and they remain off the RCMP E-PANA list of victims being investigated.

One explanation for the RCMP's exclusion of the Jack family and the eight victims from Quesnel may be found in something Staff Sergeant Bruce Hulan, team commander of Project E-PANA, told Neal Hall, a reporter with the *Vancouver Sun*, in 2009. When asked if there were other files that may be similar and could be put on the same list as those currently being investigated, Hulan said: "There are other investigations out there that when you look at them would cause you to be concerned whether there are connections between them, but as I said before, we are constrained by resources. But also I think it's important that when assigning investigators to a project, there is not necessarily a goal but an end in sight. If we bring in 100 files, it will never end. So when you give a job to a person and it's almost impossible to achieve, you start losing people pretty fast ... it's not an overwhelming list."

Hulan said that due to a lack of resources, efforts were made to control the volume of files being investigated; the entire province's files could not be examined.[23] He seemed to be indicating that a lack of RCMP resources, and a focus on concluding investigations in a timely manner to keep investigators committed, superseded the inclusion of cases that may have given investigators cause for concern. Unfortunately, this approach is of little comfort to the families of excluded victims, such as the Jack family, the Quesnel murdered and missing women, and other families of missing or murdered women throughout the province of British Columbia.

While the RCMP expanded their search for a serial killer, this search did not include the entire province, which might seem odd considering that police had to have been aware that in the 1960s and 1970s, young men and women hitchhiked along Highway 16, across the Trans-Canada Highway, throughout the United States and south to Mexico.[24] Closer to the Highway of Tears, they must have also been aware that criminals could be a geographically fluid bunch. For instance, a Victoria schoolteacher had been charged with having a sexual relationship with a former student in Prince George in the 1980s;[25] another man charged with assault causing bodily harm and using violence against a justice-system participant outside a Prince George courthouse also faced several assault charges around the Lower Mainland in the early 2000s;[26] a thirty-four-year-old male who pled guilty to charges of sexual assault causing bodily harm for an attack on a seven-year-old in Prince George in 2003 had also committed other crimes in the province of Alberta.[26] All these examples clearly illustrate that BC criminals don't necessarily stay in one place.

In fact, between 1974 and 1985 there were 329 unsolved homicides throughout all of British Columbia,[28] but in 2008 when the Victoria *Times Colonist* requested a specific list of all unsolved homicides and suspicious missing persons cases on Vancouver Island, the RCMP declined to provide the information. Their reason, their release "would compromise investigations."[29]

British Columbia's Highway of Tears problems are just a small part of an even larger Canadian tragedy. Unfortunately, no one seems to agree on an accurate figure of those murdered and missing. In 2014 the RCMP pegged the national number at 1,181 murdered and missing women. In February 2016, Patricia Hajdu, the federal Minister for the Status of Women, suggested it seemed impossible to accurately forecast the number, suggesting 4,000 might be more accurate considering what she described as a "history of police underreporting murders or failing to investigate suspicious deaths."[30] While a correct number is critical, I remained focused on the original nine Highway of Tears cases I've mentioned.

———

One or more predators on the Highway of Tears have preyed on students, a single mother, a young woman working to pay her way through university and another who was attending a local college to acquire the education needed to become employable. Yes, all but one were Aboriginal and some used drugs recreationally, as hundreds of thousands of others their age do on a casual basis. Some used drugs to escape the degradation of being trafficked as prostitutes. But more importantly, like all of us, they had parents, siblings, grandparents, aunts, uncles and friends. And like all of us, every one of them had hopes and dreams. However, through horrific, tragic circumstances, their lives were ended and the lives of their loved ones were changed forever.

For several years following the 2006 Highway of Tears Symposium, hundreds of stories about the highway appeared on television, were reported in newspapers and magazines, and were produced as documentaries. These stories made their way throughout British Columbia, across Canada, and into the United States, France, Germany and Australia. Sadly, though, during the lead-up to the 2015 Canadian federal election, you would have been hard-pressed to find many people in Greater Vancouver or the rest of Canada who remembered the Highway of Tears.

4. ARMCHAIR QUARTERBACK

"Research is to see what everybody else has seen, and to think what nobody else has thought."
— Albert Szent-Györgyi, Hungarian scientist, 1893-1986.[1]

Ex-cops make the best armchair quarterbacks when it comes to police investigations and I'm no different. In December 2005, I found myself frustrated with the way things were going with the Highway of Tears police investigation. During a late-night news broadcast, I found myself disgruntled, telling my wife that I could do a better job investigating Tamara Chipman's disappearance than the police. I'm not sure if she was serious or just tired of my opinions about police investigations, but she suggested that if I was so sure why didn't I do something about it.

I guess it would be fair to say that Tamara Chipman was the trigger and Helen Betty Osborne the inspiration for my private Highway of Tears investigation. Helen had been viciously beaten and stabbed with a screwdriver more than fifty times in The Pas, Manitoba in 1971. Her face had been smashed beyond recognition, and she was found wearing only winter boots.[2] Although I had only visited The Pas, for some reason I tried to stay current with news about the investigation. And when a 1989 article in the *Chicago Tribune,* of all places, described how the town's schools, movie theatre and bars were segregated and Natives couldn't sit in seats reserved for whites, I wasn't surprised. The *Tribune* article went on to say that the RCMP had quickly hauled in Aboriginal youths for harsh questioning, while it politely asked parents of white suspects for permission to question them. "Many Canadians were not afraid to wear their prejudices against Indians on their sleeves," it stated.[3] Sadly, back when I lived in Manitoba, I hadn't given these things much thought.

Before her death Helen had moved away from her home in Norway House, a remote community on the northern end of Lake Winnipeg. She wanted to become a teacher but the local Roman Catholic school did not teach beyond Grade 8, something she wanted to do. So in 1969 she went to the Guy Hill Residential School in Clearwater Lake, twenty-nine kilometres from The Pas. This school was run by the Roman Catholic Church and although all its students were Aboriginal, none of its teachers were. In September 1971, the Department of Indian Affairs arranged room and board for Helen in a private home in The Pas. Her body was discovered not long after that.

The initial investigation focused on her Aboriginal friends, but it stalled when investigators failed to identify her murderer. Intermittent checks were made on the case over the years until an extensive file review was done in July 1983. The lack of progress with the investigation spawned allegations by people in The Pas that not only were the police and the BC Attorney General's department guilty of "racism, neglect and indifference," but also, its local citizens. There were also suggestions that many people in town knew the identities of those responsible for Helen's murder, but chose not to say anything because they considered the matter unimportant.[4]

Helen's brutal murder was eventually solved sixteen years after her body was discovered. One of the original suspects from the initial police investigation was arrested, charged, convicted and sentenced to life in prison; one man was acquitted; and one was never charged because he was given immunity from prosecution in return for testifying against the other two. Many were asking why it took so long to bring the perpetrators to trial. Naturally, there were murmurs about Aboriginal people not being treated with the same respect as non-Aboriginals.

On April 13, 1988, almost two decades after Helen's murder, the Manitoba provincial government established the Public Inquiry into the Administration of Justice and Aboriginal People, headed by Commissioner A.C. Hamilton. The inquiry concluded Helen Betty Osborne's death "was fuelled by racism and sexism; she had fallen victim to vicious stereotypes born of ignorance and aggression." The inquiry also noted that "racism and significant errors marred the initial RCMP investigation...."[5] Unfortunately, most of the inquiry's over 150 recommendations were never acted upon.[6]

I began looking for answers and information specific to the Tear's cases at my home computer, conducting hours of open-source research (OSR). This is a powerful process also known as data mining, open-source cyber research and open-source intelligence gathering of public information—information which is available to everyone if they know where to look. Fortunately for me, and to the displeasure of the RCMP, Tony Romeyn, a local businessman and RCMP victim-services volunteer, started an Internet website detailing the Highway of Tears trail of murdered and missing women. Though of significant use, Prince George RCMP spokesman, Constable Gary Goodwin, complained that the RCMP couldn't verify the accuracy of any information that might be posted on the private website. So the RCMP came up with a solution: "Any information about missing people should be given to the police immediately. Once that information is investigated by the police, RCMP can communicate it to the public through newspaper, radio, television, and Internet media."[7] Not long after the inception of the website, the RCMP gave its creator an ultimatum: take down the site or end his fifteen-year association with the force. To his credit, Mr. Romeyn ended his long volunteer relationship with the RCMP and continued to maintain the website. Later it would be taken over by Carrier Sekani Family

Services. Unfortunately, the new website, although clean, bright and professionally designed, is not the encyclopedic resource it once was.

OSR is such a powerful tool that in 1984 the Canadian Security Intelligence Service (CSIS) decided to hire university graduates to use it to complement traditional undercover sources in efforts to analyze threats and trends, and then make recommendations to the Canadian government.[8] In fact, it is so powerful that William Studeman, former Deputy Director of the United States Central Intelligence Agency, estimated in 1992 that more than eighty percent of many intelligence needs could be met through open sources.[9] The RCMP too acknowledged in 2002 that they found the web a valuable tool,[10] and a decade later a senior RCMP investigator said that open-source research is now a standard component of many criminal investigations.[11]

OSR might sound complex, but it's not rocket science. On the other hand, it is time-consuming. Every time you do a Google search, check out someone's Twitter, Facebook or other online account for information, search eBay for a used car or look for your soulmate on a dating website, you are conducting OSR. I have no illusions about the importance of the work I do compared to CSIS, the CIA or, for that matter, the RCMP, but I do know the intelligence I obtain from OSR is a very important part of every one of my company's investigations. I use it to obtain the names of property owners; identify tenants; check for criminal charges; locate and link telephone numbers to individuals; link individuals to one another; find coworkers, friends, neighbours and lovers; search newspaper databases; conduct real-estate analysis; and locate people. As an example, I once used OSR to find a surveillance target—PI jargon meaning the individual I was planning to observe closely. Up until then he had been successfully hiding from people like me. Unfortunately for him, he made the mistake of trying to return a lost pet to its owner by putting a post on a veterinarian's lost-and-found site. In the posting, my target described the area in which he lived as it related to a nearby intersection. Once I arrived at the intersection, I used it as the centre of my street search and slowly moved outward, increasing the circumference of the area I searched as I went along. I found my target's vehicle parked in the driveway of his previously unknown home in less than an hour. It's no wonder police departments often research media reports and other OSR data to help spot links in cases.[12]

OSR can also be gathered in person from unlikely sources such as news reporters, city officials, municipal employees—basically anyone who will talk to you. Others, such as police investigators and their associates, won't, but if you happen to be at the right place at the right time, they may unintentionally reveal details of an investigation over lunch, coffee or a beer after work. Early in my

Tears investigation, on one of my trips to Prince George, I found myself standing in a group of airline passengers waiting for our luggage to be unloaded from the plane. As I surveyed the group of people who had just arrived from Vancouver, I recognized the RCMP officer in charge of the province's Major Crime Unit and, ultimately, the Highway of Tears investigation. He was on the other side of the room talking to a fellow officer. Since I knew they wouldn't recognize me, I manoeuvred to a position directly behind them which allowed me to easily eavesdrop on their conversation. In another instance I learned cause of death details of one of the Tears victims simply because I talked to someone who had found herself sitting at a table next to the men having that conversation during lunch. This information was not publicly known and was previously unknown to me. In all probability, it was considered the case's holdback information, or information that is only known to police and the murderer and for that reason, not made public.

Both of these examples were chance encounters, but OSR opportunities can also be planned. Once you've identified the individual you hope to get information from, and as long as your identity is unknown, the rest is relatively easy. This individual could be a police officer, lawyer, Crown prosecutor, your client's husband or wife's hairdresser. Once you know your target, all you have to do is identify their favourite coffee shop or eatery, or a neighbourhood pub they regularly frequent. The smaller the city or town, the easier it is to uncover the haunts of creatures of habit.

If it's the police you are interested in, look for police cars, both marked and unmarked, parked outside restaurants during lunch or coffee breaks. Or locate those coffee shops located within walking distance of a police office. Cops choose their hangouts for many reasons: good-looking bussers, ample parking, proximity to a precinct, and—because many cops are cheap—places offering good food at reasonable prices, or better, one that serves them free coffee. Once they've found a favourite location they are in and out of it like a revolving door, and once you've located that hangout and identified their behavioural patterns, all you have to do is park outside and wait until they show up. You can then follow them in and once they're seated at a table, usually a favourite table, you can sit as close to them as possible, order a coffee, get out your notebook and prepare to listen and learn. For example, Mounties in Prince George used to leave their office on coffee break using a well-travelled route: they made their way down a back lane, then through a narrow driveway below the skyway of the motel next door, then jaywalked across the street to either Tim Hortons or White Spot just a short walk away.

All said, some of my early OSR research revealed that in 1995, Bob Paulson, an RCMP corporal from Prince Rupert Sub-Division who would eventually become the commissioner of the RCMP, organized a Prince George conference of RCMP investigators, crime analysts and psychological profilers to determine if a serial killer was roaming the area.[13] The group looked into the disappearances of five First Nations girls that occurred between 1990 and 1995. They concluded that three of the cases appeared to have involved the same killer. The three related victims were Ramona Wilson, Roxanne Thiara and Leah Germaine.[14] Despite this, Terrace RCMP Corporal Rob McKay told the media that although you could say all victims were young Native girls and all cases originated in the northern or northwestern region of the province, he dismissed a serial killer theory saying: "That's pretty generic to try to link something like this together." As well, Corporal Paulson said the Mounties were concerned that there was a serial killer and had done everything they could do to investigate, but added, "the possibility still exists that these were separate incidents."[15]

By the end of January 2006, I was thoroughly committed to my investigation and had completed hundreds of hours of OSR. I also came up with my first working theory, that Roxanne Thiara's and Alishia Germaine's murders and perhaps Nicole Hoar's disappearance were the work of a serial killer. Now it was time to identify potential witnesses or those that might have information. I decided to capitalize on a fact of life in the criminal world: that is, if you are going to do the crime you damn well better be prepared to do the time because everyone from your mother, your wife, brother and anyone you've ever worked for or with in the past are potential informants against you—and it's been my experience that it's not difficult to get them to talk.

To start—and against the urging of a good friend who suggested if I wanted to waste my money I should just give it to him instead—I placed a small card-sized notice in the *Terrace Standard* in February 2006.

MURDERED OR MISSING

If you have any information regarding anything odd or unusual happening, or someone acting strangely in relation to any of the 7 murdered or missing women along Highway 16 and HAVE NOT already done so, please call the RCMP or Crime Stoppers today!

If you are too intimidated to call or want to remain anonymous
to the authorities, please call or email Ray
in confidence at Valley Pacific Investigations Ltd.

vpi@telusmail.net • vpi@telusmail.net
If you are too intimidated to call or want to remain anonymous to the authorities,
please call or email Ray, in confidence at Valley Pacific Investigations Ltd.
vpi@telusmail.net • vpi@telusmail.net

I had hoped this would generate a few calls. Instead, it unleashed a torrent of them. Once I started talking to people, once I put my feet on the ground, I quickly discovered that the number-one complaint potential police tipsters had, and continue to have today, was the difficulty they experienced passing along information to a real cop, let alone getting that information into the hands of real Tears case investigators. Invariably, callers would end up talking to a civilian in the police office or a civilian call-taker at Crime Stoppers. When they were successfully able to get in touch with an actual cop, they were almost always unfamiliar with the case and it soon became clear their sole purpose was to pass tipsters off to someone else, often someone out of the area and a long-distance call away. To make matters worse, many First Nations residents who live along Highway 16 have no long-distance telephone service, so they were forced to call Prince George from their reserve's band office. Their call would be met by an answering machine where they would leave a message for investigators, but there was no realistic way for a cop to call the tipster back because it would have been akin to calling a payphone.

It seemed the RCMP didn't appreciate the fact that it takes great courage for members of the noncriminal public to call the police, and it takes even more courage for those on the fringe or within the criminal subculture to do it. Once a person on the margins of society is brushed off, the chances of that person following through again diminish substantially.

In fall 2009, a toll-free Unsolved Homicide Tip Line (1-877-543-4822) for "E" Division RCMP was available for tipsters or in other words, for all of BC. When I called there recently on a Saturday morning I got an answering machine. This surprised me because it would be very simple to call-forward that number, on a rotation basis, to any one of the dozens of RCMP members working homicide cases throughout the province. Callers would then have the opportunity to talk to a real cop. I re-called the number in May 2016. It was still in service and still operating as an answering machine. Criminals and their associates have a very personal and often unpleasant history with police. As a result, in the same way they are stereotyped by police *they* also stereotype the police. These stereotypes include concepts about cookie-cutter cop behaviour, huge egos and self-perceived superiority. If a criminal senses rightly or wrongly any such stereotypical behaviour, including conduct that is inconsiderate, demeaning and bullying, they turn off, completely. When members of the public, including criminals, decide to give police information and are humiliated in the process, intimidated or simply brushed off, they will never call the police again—about anything.

Bad-experience stories involving people who tried to help the RCMP constantly circulate throughout entire Tears communities. Marketing gurus will tell you it's a generally accepted fact that one person will relate their bad experience to ten others, who tell ten, who tell ten others and so on. Right or wrong, these stories are out there, and they do impact on those who might be able to provide information to police. This might explain why an organization like

Terrace Crime Stoppers, for instance, paid out $1,400 in 2004, down to $450 in 2005 and, with only two months left in 2006, had not paid out any money to any of the forty-six tipsters who called that year.[16]

Crime Stoppers is an independent non-profit society managed by a civilian board of directors. Its purpose is to work in partnership with police, the media and local citizenry by providing a vehicle which allows citizens to anonymously supply police with information about a crime. If the information leads to an arrest and charge, the individual could receive a reward of up to $2,000 without ever being identified or having to go to court. Unfortunately, one Terrace Crime Stoppers board member may have hurt the cause by characterizing potential callers as people with little information yet were expecting to collect $2,000 for the tip.[17] Here's the problem: a person calling, for example, to say they saw a truck at a crime scene may not be providing enough information to secure an arrest or conviction. While it's true that more information is better, and the truck's make, model, colour, licence plate number, and a cellphone picture of the vehicle and its occupants along with detailed police-type notes would be preferred, there is an old saying that's appropriate here: "Don't look a gift horse in the mouth." Sometimes just knowing a truck and not a car was used during the commission of a crime may just be the clue needed to include or eliminate a potential suspect.

If it's true that ninety percent of all crimes in Canada are solved with information given by tipsters or involved citizens,[18] and a Crime Stoppers organization along the Highway of Tears is receiving few if any calls, that organization should be asking why it's not receiving calls rather than insulting the few who do take the time to phone in.

Frankly, I know how these callers must feel. As mentioned, when I first started my investigation I made a point of stopping into RCMP detachments along the Highway of Tears to introduce myself and explain what I was up to, only to be met with silence. In the really old days, the staff sergeant in charge of the detachment would have wanted to talk to a guy like me, to find out firsthand what I was up to and make it clear what his expectations were of me, much the same way Terrace Staff Sergeant Eric Stubbs did after a newspaper story was written about my negative experience with the RCMP. Stubbs telephoned me, suggesting I should have expressed my concerns directly to him and not the local media so we could have quietly resolved the issue. He was subsequently short of words when I explained that a week earlier, I had attended his office looking for him but he was out. I left my business card with a civilian employee and requested that the employee tell the detachment commander I had dropped by, would be in town for a few days, and would like to talk to him. He never got my card or my message. Months later, when the RCMP finally decided to communicate with me and I was able to pass along information, I was never re-contacted, so for all I know my information went into their trash bin unread.

That said, I was starting to generate more and more leads. In fact I no longer had to pay for newspaper notices asking for help because my involvement was getting more and more attention in the news. Unfortunately, there was a downside to all this free publicity: I started to worry about how much quiet attention I was receiving from the RCMP as my public profile increased. By nature police are a sneaky bunch, whether using contrived self-positioning to climb the corporate ladder; hiding in the weeds at a radar trap; dressing as a construction worker to catch cellphone cheaters; or using every resource at their disposal to discredit and sideline those who obstruct their way of doing things. I knew I had awakened a sleeping giant the day I received a phone call from a northern newspaper reporter who told me the staff sergeant in charge of the local detachment showed up looking for a copy of the paper containing one of my "murdered or missing" notices.

Up to this time my calls to the RCMP had gone unanswered. I had been picking up rumours and gossip along Highway 16 regarding a multitude of local criminals and criminal non-Tears activities I thought worthy of their attention. This included information involving the names of local drug dealers, methods of drug distribution between Vancouver and Northern British Columbia, and the name of a motel that may have been a hot-spot of sexual exploitation. I heard stories about pimps, prostitutes and, in one case, a police file which supposedly went missing from a locked RCMP detachment filing cabinet, resulting in the dismissal of drug charges against two men. Although this information was generated from gossip and rumours which, like seeds planted in a new garden that can either dry up and die or grow and mature, for investigators it can be information needed to move a case along. Over time I also realized something very valuable. The gossip, rumours and names of participants in serious local criminal activity, received from Native people for the most part, proved to be extremely accurate. I don't know why I was surprised. I know locals in any community can be the eyes and ears for the police—that is, if police have the public's trust and are interested in receiving their help. I, however, was very fortunate because I had somehow gained the trust of many people in First Nations communities all along the Highway of Tears, and I was humbled.

As I began generating more and more tips, those tips in turn began to generate more and more interest from the northern media who were keeping the public interested in the Highway of Tears. Unfortunately, all this attention was starting to make me nervous. Not because I had something to hide. Instead, I was starting to lose my anonymity, something that threatened my personal safety. But it was more than that. I was nervous because I had "poked the bear," the RCMP.

I continued to conduct counter-surveillance after work before returning to my motel for the night, but it became more intense and calculated. Simply put, surveillance is the process of watching an individual's movements for a pre-determined purpose, criminal or otherwise. Counter-surveillance, on the other hand, would be conducted to find out if you are the target of surveillance, and to identify those who are conducting it so you can protect yourself or otherwise act accordingly. I was used to working alone, coming and going surreptitiously; often even my wife had no idea where my investigation was taking me or who I was talking to.

Regarding the media, I wasn't looking for my fifteen minutes, but started taking advantage of the opportunity to talk to them whenever I could because it resulted in more and more newspaper stories. In turn the stories not only generated dozens of tips, but also kept the Tears tragedy fresh in the eyes of the public, the politicians and—unfortunately for me—senior RCMP managers.

Up to this time, the RCMP's northern *non*-managerial members and criminal investigators seemed to have no problem with my attempts to help with their Tears investigation. In fact, some investigators had passed along information, and an ex-investigator went so far as to let me sneak a peek at his notes. In Prince George, a local RCMP member told the public via the media that although the police had significant manpower working the cases, a private investigation might help police by "raising case profiles."[19] This member said the police appreciated my efforts because the more people out there looking and listening, the better.[20]

That said, in September 2006, Rena Zatorski, Lheidli T'enneh Nation councillor in Prince George, suggested to the *Prince George Free Press* that it appeared the RCMP had increased their efforts to solve the Highway of Tears cases, likely a result of their own embarrassment in the face of public pressure; she also suggested that maybe it was going to take a private investigator to make more headway than the Mounties.[21]

Now the RCMP was being publicly poked by the Aboriginal community, in part because of what I was doing. After a newspaper article quoted me as saying I had the names of five persons of interest in regard to the Highway of Tears crimes, the result of telephone tips I'd received, "E" Division Communications Officer John Ward said the RCMP would "talk to me and make sure the lines of communication were open."[22] In fact John and I had previously worked together in North Vancouver. He had come directly from a drug-squad operation in the East and was assigned to our municipal detachment. We became friends. I remember telling my wife that although I appreciated that he had publicly acknowledged me, I felt bad for him because he would soon regret it.

Not long after this I had my first informal meeting with the RCMP, in a coffee shop, orchestrated by Staff Sergeant Hulan, the Mountie in charge of the British Columbia Unsolved Homicide Unit and head of Project E-PANA, the Highway of Tears investigative unit. I got the impression that the staff sergeant was expecting me to come to my senses and immediately remove myself from the investigation as quietly and uneventfully as possible. When that didn't happen, my old friend, the province's RCMP communications officer, was tasked with giving me a public scolding in a northern newspaper. In an effort to distance himself, he referred to me as "that gentleman, Mr. Michalko" (they rarely referred to me as a licenced private investigator), explaining to the public that I was to share any leads I got so the RCMP could take it from there. I suspect the RCMP thought if the public were given the impression that I had been ordered to turn over all information to the police, then there was no longer any reason for a citizen to call me. Problem was, callers who wanted to remain anonymous would realize their anonymity was at stake and now would never call me. Lost here was the fact that they were phoning me because they didn't trust the police. Apparently, it was okay to scare off future informants than benefit from the work of a now-trusted PI. My old friend suggested that the RCMP, who had been working on these cases for some time, could investigate more easily than a private investigator because of their status as professional police officers, major crime investigators with behavioural experts, forensic experts and DNA experts. He sarcastically concluded that "he didn't know if I had that kind of support behind me."[23] The RCMP was behaving like a bully in the school yard, with the attitude that if they couldn't get the information, neither should I.

Although I was troubled by his new approach, I knew my old friend was just covering his ass. He was under pressure from his superiors. Many would say he really had no choice but to try to discredit me, but I don't know. It reminded me of the unofficial RCMP motto that recruits were given during training in the 1960s: "There is a right way of doing things, a wrong way of doing things, and the Royal Canadian Mounted Police way of doing things." This attitude was still alive and well and, as in the past, God help those who forgot it.

After hearing an interview I did on CBC Radio One in 2006, a number of Vancouver people, the majority of which were women, volunteered to raise money to help cover some of my hard costs such as airline travel and car rental. They managed to raise slightly more than $7,000 which helped alleviate some of these expenses. With the cost of one trip north averaging between $800 to $1,000, these funds made it easier to continue my investigation. This bright spot aside, I continued to be bothered by my old friend, John Ward. Six days after his first media account of me, he was back at it, telling the media I clearly understood the importance of following protocol which involved sharing leads with the RCMP and not revealing any case details to the public. This time he referred to me as a former RCMP member. The *Lakes District News* in Burns Lake described Ward's attitude as defensive, the result of bruised RCMP egos and an attempt to show that the RCMP was in charge—a declaration of authority by the RCMP I guess, which would almost certainly cause more stress on relations between First Nations and police detachments in the missing girls communities around the province.[24]

I decided to defend my position with a letter to the editor of *The Interior News* in Smithers. I began by noting that as a private investigator I had no power of arrest, so the only option open was to turn my leads over to police. I repeated what I had been trying to say since I first became involved. The RCMP indeed have the training, investigative skill and resources necessary to solve these crimes and missing person cases, which begs the question: Why, with all their expertise and resources, have the RCMP been unable to solve any? I told readers that finding a police officer who was willing to establish a real dialogue and working relationship with me had been an ongoing problem from the start. It had taken the RCMP seven months for someone to contact me to establish a line of communication, and

I concluded by writing that my old friend should turn his soapbox around and give the lecture to his own members.[25]

What I didn't realize at the time was that my friend's public stance on the issue, together with my rebuttal, would turn out to be the single biggest boost to my investigation. And how ironic was it that it came directly from the RCMP's attempts to discredit me. Up until our exchange, I was making some headway but I got the impression many people along the Highway of Tears saw me as just another "one of the (RCMP) boys," albeit in the form of an ex-member. Soon after the paper hit the newsstands I got a call from an Aboriginal friend who lived on a reserve in Northern BC. She told me she and her husband had read the Mountie's comments and my rebuttal, as had other members of their community, and they were especially not impressed with the attitude of the police. Although it was by accident, with no planning on my part, the public immediately took me off the "He's one of the RCMP old boys" list and put me on the "He's just like us, the police don't like him either" list. This turned out to be a huge factor in my ability to further gain the trust of strangers, and the calls started flooding in like never before. Not only that but by mid-November 2006 over 1,000 articles about the Highway of Tears had appeared in media sources and various publications throughout Canada, with dozens more appearing in a handful of countries around the world. The more negative the RCMP were toward me, the more people trusted me.

I ended 2006 by distributing flyers about the Highway of Tears to all federal and provincial prisons, asking for help. The following year I received a call from an inmate. When I went to the facility to visit the prisoner, I was happily surprised to find a number of my flyers taped to the stark cement walls. I was able to pass the information I received there along to the RCMP, though was later given the impression that they considered it more about the prisoner hoping for some fresh air than it was about passing on credible information.

In May 2007 Clarence and Lorraine Joseph, a First Nations couple, found a backpack, a pair of women's jeans, some black lingerie and an undergarment dumped beside an old logging road west of Moricetown on Highway 16. They called Smithers RCMP. Two weeks later the couple returned to the site where, to their surprise, they found the backpack and clothing still there, just as they had initially found it. On the evening of Tuesday, May 8th I received a telephone call about the uninvestigated clothes and called Smithers RCMP the following morning. I was told there had been some internal disagreement with a neighbouring RCMP detachment as to whether the site was located in Hazelton or Smithers. As a result, the original call was not investigated as quickly as it should have been. Three days later the clothes were still onsite and nothing had been done by Smithers RCMP, so the couple took a Smithers *Interior* newspaper reporter there. Another thirty metres into the forest, two more piles of clothing were found. Smithers RCMP said they had passed the file on to another detachment two weeks prior. Sergeant Todd Scott, from Hazelton RCMP, confirmed this, but officers were unable to find the location or contact the Josephs.[26] Smithers RCMP said they had alerted the Highway of Tears Task Force about the clothing and the RCMP's provincial spokesperson said the Prince George Major Crime Unit had been called to examine it.[27] Up to this time many women and girls had been murdered or had gone missing along this stretch of highway. Under the circumstances, where on Earth would a pile of discarded women's clothing not be a priority to police?

Unfortunately, this was not the first story I heard about the RCMP's handling of found clothing. The first was from a Smithers couple whose dog showed up in the yard one day with what appeared to be a piece of bloody clothing. Thinking their pet's discovery might be significant, they called the local detachment and a member was dispatched to pick up the find. They later learned that the clothing they had given the constable never made it back to the police office and was either lost or discarded, as if it were somehow irrelevant.

5. THE COPS, THE COURTS AND THE CHURCH

"Mistrust created a wall of silence that's gone on for generations and now hurts both sides. It even makes it tough to solve crimes when nobody will talk to you."
— Anishinaabe (Ojibwa), Colleen Simard, a writer and columnist for the *Winnipeg Free Press*

Good investigators have the ability to make use of all available tools and there is no better tool for police in any investigation than local community members, those people who shared experiences with the victims. And these experience can be of any kind—personal, cultural, geographical, social, whatever. In terms of the Highway of Tears, this means Native people. Sadly, there is a three-headed monster on the Highway of Tears that has eroded the trust of locals and turned potential informants against those who are in a position to help—and this unholy trinity is the Cops, Courts and the Church. Together they've managed to turn many in these northern communities against them, and in so doing have perhaps hampered the RCMP's ability to solve any of these cases.

Cops need informants, or at the very least people who trust them enough to offer help in the way of information. But cops were considered henchmen collectors during the Sixties Scoop where thousands of Native children were taken from their families and placed in foster homes or put up for adoption. And the memory of this—and all the related residual effects—have not faded up here.

Not by a long shot. Couple this with the role the RCMP played in forcing children into residential schools—and the trust divide only widens.

But it gets worse. There are specific issues between police and Natives that push the divide even further. In Yorkton, Saskatchewan, for instance, a First Nations woman received an out-of-court settlement from the RCMP after she was detained in a cell for almost fifteen hours, stripped of her underwear, and denied water.[1] In northern Manitoba an RCMP member took an intoxicated woman he had arrested, out of lock-up, to her home to pursue a relationship. Later the senior officer in the detachment justified his cohort's behaviour by saying: "You arrested her, you can do whatever the f--k you want to do."[2] And in Saskatchewan, an RCMP officer described members of the Sucker River reserve on Facebook as: "Drunk uneducated animals shooting at each other."[3] Many Aboriginal people living along the Highway of Tears can regale you with stories and personal experiences as bad as these. And it's this continual repeating of history that has helped shape Native-police relations. When you look at it closely, it's a history of distrust and dislike.

There are other reasons cops aren't trusted. One, they often don't make marginalized people, many of whom are Native, a priority. Criminologist Dr. John Winterdyk argues that when it comes to Canadian murder cases, the police may not take all that great an interest in solving cases involving victims who belong on "the fringe." According to Winterdyk, those cases are taken less seriously by police because society places less pressure on cops to solve them. [4,5]

An example close to home that illustrates Dr. Winterdyk's theory involves the police investigation into the abduction of a young Vancouver man, the son of a millionaire taken from the upscale Southlands area just a few kilometres away from his family's $3.8-million mansion.[6] According to police, in April 2006 hundreds of officers, including members from the RCMP, the FBI, Scotland Yard, and others worked 24/7 on the investigation. This high-profile search led one reporter to conclude that the case was handled much differently by police, politicians and the public than the cases of dozens of women that had been murdered or gone missing from Vancouver's Downtown Eastside or Highway 16.[7] Nevertheless, when the twenty-four-year-old Southlands kidnapping victim was eventually discovered alive, Vancouver City Police Chief Jamie Graham said: "You get one of these cases in a career."[8]

When interviewed, Corporal Peter Cross, a senior investigator in the Surrey RCMP homicide unit, spoke about policing in his region. But his take on the matter seems to ring true across the province. His said that resources for major police investigations often depend on how deep public interest runs and the willingness of politicians to provide adequate funds. For example, in 2001 the Surrey RCMP spent approximately $1 million searching for and then arresting a suspect in the murder of ten-year-old Heather Thomas, a case Cross described as "one which touched BC residents." A year later while working on a prostitution-related investigation, Cross had to carefully account for all the money spent on the investigation. While sympathizing with his budget-conscious bosses, Cross believed there should be enough money available to treat each murder case equally, regardless of the victim's background.[9]

More specific to the Tears investigation, the *Highway of Tears Symposium Recommendation Report* released in 2006 also supported Dr. Winterdyk's theory, noting that the 2002 disappearance of Nicole Hoar—the only white victim to date—made the term "Highway of Tears" much more widely known. At the same time, many along Highway 16 considered the high-profile investigation into Nicole's disappearance not nearly on level with cases involving Aboriginal women, street people, individuals involved in high-risk activities and others "on the fringe."

Other forms of police conduct also undermine Native-police trust relations. In Prince George in 1989, for instance, a police investigation into a judge's sex-related offences involving teenage Aboriginal girls identified nine police officers and members of the justice system, including a lawyer, as having had sex with prostitutes.[10] Internal allegations were made, however the disciplinary charges were dropped later because the RCMP waited too long to launch their case.[11] In September the reputation of the RCMP took another hit when a study conducted by the Prince George New Hope Society indicated that sixty-three women and forty-three girls said they had been asked for sex by an RCMP officer and were otherwise also mistreated by the force. Dahl Chambers, superintendent and operations officer in charge of the Prince George detachment, said he'd "love to see the complaints," commenting: "If you accuse someone, you have to follow through, so the misconduct could be fully investigated."[12] Indeed, but the question that became clear to all who followed the news was still not addressed: How can these women expect to be treated fairly knowing their complaint *about* the RCMP will be investigated *by* the RCMP?

To get a better idea how locals feel about the RCMP one just has to look at how the force responded to questions about their involvement in the 2006 shooting and subsequent death of Ian Bush in the Highway of Tears community of Smithers. When responding to the issue their media relations representative simply said: "The public doesn't have a right to know anything."[13]

In 2011 the BC Civil Liberties Association (BCCLA) released *Small Town Justice: A report on the RCMP in Northern and Rural*

British Columbia, which was described as a "temperature-taking of the public mood around the RCMP in fourteen rural and northern communities." One of the most telling remarks made by a survey participant in Prince George was: "It's hard to tell your kids to trust the RCMP when you have a hard time trusting them." The report showed that Smithers respondents believed that the RCMP seemed to be "only answerable to themselves." Furthermore, another participant believed that the RCMP was out to "protect themselves." One survey participant also suggested that to capture RCMP community relations, Aboriginal youth should "hang out in a zone where there is local video surveillance that captures RCMP conduct towards them."[14]

But it's not just the RCMP, it's the legal system as well. In the paper *Aboriginal Peoples and the Criminal Justice System*, Jonathan Ruden, writing for the Ipperwash Inquiry, defined over-policing as "the practice of police targeting people of particular ethnic or racial backgrounds or people who live in particular neighbourhoods." Ruden also wrote that: "While Aboriginal people are clearly over-policed today, over-policing has a particular history with regards to Aboriginal people." The result is massive imprisonment of Native people to the point where the Supreme Court of Canada concluded that overrepresentation of Aboriginal people in the prison system is a "crisis in the Canadian judicial system."[15]

But it's not just "the system." Sometimes it's the judges themselves. For instance, Mary Clifford, the Prince George Native Friendship Centre's health director, said she filed a report with the RCMP after she saw a teenage Aboriginal girl sitting in a parked car with a Judge David Ramsay at the wheel. Ramsey was talking with an RCMP officer. The following day Mary went to the RCMP to make a complaint, and when the Mountie taking her complaint saw the judge's name she said: "His eyeballs shot open!" Ms. Clifford never heard anything back from the RCMP but said she was told by some unidentified Mounties that they knew the judge was "'preying on kids but they couldn't get their superiors to act." When asked about these rumours, RCMP Staff Sergeant John Ward said: "We're not in the business of confirming what people are saying on the streets."[16]

That said, in June of 2004, Provincial Court Judge David Ramsay was sentenced to seven years in prison after pleading guilty to four violent sexual offences involving girls as young as twelve.[17] Presiding B.C. Supreme Court Associate Chief Judge Patrick Dohm said: "I find it impossible to believe Ramsay developed these appalling appetites a year after he was appointed to the provincial court bench in his late 40s." Judge Dohm also said: "I am also incredulous about the RCMP taking three years to nail him. It sounds to me like the force didn't give it the priority it demanded—and the public deserves to know why."[18]

So, if Native people and other potential tipsters and informants along Highway 16 and elsewhere can't trust the police or the legal system in general, who can they turn to. Traditionally Native people have often turned to churches whose priests have competed for their souls for centuries—but to what damage to Native customs and community? As we now know, the residential school system—a collaborative social experiment orchestrated by the courts and carried out by police and church—was such a tragic abuse at every level that to regain the widespread trust of Aboriginals would take a miracle.

Unfortunately, cases of the church acting badly can be found even today. What has been described as a "miscommunication" by a federal lawyer paved the way for the Catholic Church to wiggle out of its $25-million obligation to compensate survivors of residential schools,[19] a move more in line with the 1800s than today.

But no matter, because local examples of church betrayal abound here as well. Take Hubert Patrick O'Connor, the Roman Catholic Bishop of Whitehorse who in 1986 was named Bishop of Prince George, with the authority to run the diocese in and around the city.[20] A decade later he was charged with sexual and indecent assault of two young First Nations girls—crimes which had occurred thirty years earlier. At the time of his conviction, he was the highest-ranking Catholic in the world to be found guilty of sex offences.[21] The disgraced priest died in 2007 and was buried in the Oblates of Mary Immaculate Cemetery in Mission, British Columbia.[22]

All successful investigations rely on a steady stream of information from members of the community, which include potential witnesses, tipsters, informants, friends, relatives, neighbours, street people, homeless people. The list goes on and on. Yet it's very clear that many of these people along Highway 16 (and elsewhere) have been alienated by the cops, court and church. In that light and to have any success with these murdered and missing women's cases, I would have to be considered an outsider, someone sympathetic to the public's point of view.

6. THE DEVIL WALKS AMONG US

"Meetings are indispensable when you don't want to do anything."
— John Kenneth Galbraith

The idea for a Highway of Tears Symposium originated with the Lheidli T'enneh First Nation, whose traditional territory stretches over 4.3 million hectares from the Alberta border to north-central British Columbia.[1] It was organized by the Lheidli T'enneh, along with Carrier Sekani Family Services, the Carrier Sekani Tribal Council, the Prince George Friendship Centre, and the Prince George Nechako Aboriginal Employment and Training Association. It took place in Prince George on March 30 and 31, 2006.

In the lead-up to the symposium, the BC Ministry of Public Safety and Solicitor General issued a news release noting that over thirty-five RCMP officers were dedicated to the Highway of Tears cases.[2] Lheidli T'enneh Nation's councillor, Rena Zatorski, said Aboriginal people in general were unhappy and angry with the RCMP because they had no idea what, if anything, they were doing.[3] No wonder, not one case had been solved in decades.

Ms. Zatorski explained part of the problem on a "disconnect" between police and Aboriginal youth, some of whom tend to fall into dangerous lifestyles that can lead to problems. Then in a rare public assertion by an Aboriginal politician, she said it was up to the Aboriginal leadership and communities to deal with such issues.[4] Ben Meisner, veteran Prince George newsman, and owner and host of the Internet radio show and blogsite *Opinion 250*, agreed, saying that millions of dollars on inquiries will not change the reality that people living along Highway 16 "better get off their seats and do something about the dangerous practice of (hitchhiking)" rather than waiting for someone else to come along and fix the problem.[5]

When I first started to hear talk about the upcoming Highway of Tears Symposium in early 2006, I was skeptical. I knew it might be a good way for some of the victims' families to meet and share their stories in an effort to heal, but I thought it wouldn't provide us with any new information. Nevertheless, the symposium would bring together the who's who of British Columbia's Aboriginal and non-Aboriginal politicians, bureaucrats, senior RCMP members, and special interest groups, all of whom shared at least some blame for the root causes up here, and all of whom would use the symposium to show the world that they were taking the problem seriously. In other words, they would be covering their collective asses.

The symposium was billed as a "community call for action." It attracted ninety organizations and 500 delegates. John Les, Solicitor General and British Columbia's top law enforcement official, was in attendance. He described the symposium as a time of coming together in the wake of tragic circumstances and a way to ask what could be done to make Highway 16 safe again.

Also in attendance were Stan Hagen, Minister of Children and Family Development; Nathan Cullen, Member of Parliament representing the Skeena-Bulkley Valley; a number of members from the BC Legislative Assembly, including North Coast MLA Gary Coons; Beverly Jacobs, President of the Native Women's Association of Canada; Grand Chief Edward John from the First Nations Summit; Chief Stewart Phillip of the Union of BC Indian Chiefs; Lillian George and David Dennis of the United Native Nations; Charlene Belleau of the Assembly of First Nations; and Angela Sterritt, representing Justice for Girls.[6]

The RCMP attended with the intention of outlining the status of their investigation and meeting with family members of victims.[7] To that end, senior Mounties were present, including the deputy criminal operations officer in British Columbia responsible for Community, Contract and Aboriginal Policing in the province; the officer in charge of "E" Division (British Columbia); the officer in charge of North District Major Crimes; and the officer in charge of Prince George detachment. However, this top-heavy RCMP contingent did not include any RCMP investigators, the men and women tasked with making good on their bosses' promises.

Every single individual in this group of elite British Columbians had to have already known that if you were an Aboriginal person living in British Columbia, your standard of living was likely to be twenty percent below the provincial average; that Aboriginal women and children under age fifteen suffer disproportionally high rates of violence and abuse; and forty-one percent of Aboriginal children live in families with incomes under $20,000, compared to seventeen percent for other BC children;[8] and although approximately eighty percent of Canadian households own at least one automobile, the low-income ten percent (this group) don't drive because they don't own a vehicle.[9]

This elite group should also have been aware of the 2003 *United Nations Convention on the Elimination of All Forms of Discrimination Against Women Report*, which found that Canada overall was not living up to its obligations. It specifically targeted BC, noting it was unacceptable that in a country as wealthy as Canada, forty-three percent of Aboriginal women lived in poverty.[10]

Further, the group should have been aware of the October 2004 Amnesty International report *Stolen Sisters: Discrimination and Violence Against Indigenous Women in Canada*, which cited a shocking 1996 federal statistic that Native women between twenty-five and forty-four were five times more likely to die as a result of violence than other women in the same age group. Amnesty

International reminded Canadian officials that they have a clear and inescapable obligation to ensure the safety of Indigenous women, to bring those responsible for attacks against them to justice, and to address the deeper problems of marginalization, dispossession and impoverishment which have placed so many Indigenous women in harm's way.[11]

———

Wearing a yellow reflective vest with her daughter's name emblazoned across the back, Matilda Wilson, mother of slain Ramona Wilson, walked into the Prince George auditorium to the sound of Native drums to open the Highway of Tears Symposium. Her address to the gathering was described by one reporter as evangelical. "The devil walks among us in so many ways," she said, declaring that the people or person responsible for these crimes will be caught. She closed with the words: "God have mercy on his soul."[12] It was a powerful start.

BC Solicitor General John Les told attendees he thought it was generally understood that the police were doing their best, nevertheless people felt a sense of abandonment by authorities and this concern needed to be addressed. He concluded by saying it was his responsibility to provide resources and assured the audience that RCMP officers on the cases were some of the best anywhere at solving homicides.[13]

The superintendent in charge of Prince George detachment said the RCMP's role at the symposium was to help community groups better understand how police handle cases like those of the missing and murdered women along Highway 16.[14] Staff sergeant in charge of "E" Division Media Relations, John Ward, said police were looking at the cases with an open mind. That said, John Les, BC's Solicitor General, believed it was still too early for the police to conclude a serial killer was involved in the murders or disappearances. But according to the staff sergeant, the cases were difficult to investigate because of a lack of witnesses and the fact that the perpetrators had capitalized on the remoteness of the area to commit crimes along this lonely stretch of highway.[15]

The RCMP participated in the informal workshops with Aboriginal groups, tribal leaders, and family members who had lost children or relatives on the highway. They committed to keeping family members better informed about the status of the investigations in future. Nathan Cullen, a New Democratic Party MP, concluded the Mounties had a lot of work to do to rebuild trust with Aboriginals who live along Highway 16.[17]

After attending the symposium in Prince George, Superintendent Leon Van De Walle, the RCMP officer in charge of "E" Division

Major Crime Unit, said he was interested in opening a dedicated tip line to gather Highway of Tears information. He advised a system similar to the Amber Alert program, "reserved for abductions involving children with a specific suspect or vehicle description." Van De Walle in fact went so far as to suggest that a sizable reward be offered for information given.[18] However, the dedicated tip line or reward never materialized.[19]

On June 26, 2006, after being vetted by police and victims' family members,[20] the thirty-eight-page *Highway of Tears Symposium Report* was released. Authored by First Nations consultant Don Sabo and described as "a collective voice for the victims who have been silenced," it outlined a number of short- and long-term goals. There were also thirty-two recommendations, ten of which are important to note here:

Recommendation #1—That a shuttle-bus transportation system be established between each town and city located along the entire length of Highway 16, defined as the Highway of Tears.

Recommendation #2—That while the RCMP does a commendable job in patrolling the highway, these patrols can no longer drive past a hitchhiker who fits the victim profile. Any RCMP highway patrol that encounters a hitchhiker who falls within the victim profile must stop, conduct a person check, and provide the hitchhiker with a Highway of Tears information pamphlet and a schedule of the shuttle bus between the town and city they are located at. Furthermore, the RCMP patrol should encourage the hitchhiker to wait for the shuttle bus, or next mode of transportation listed under recommendation #4.

Recommendation #3—That the RCMP be provided the resources to increase their highway patrols during the hitchhiking season, more specifically increase these patrols along the sections of Highway 16 near First Nations communities, towns and cities. Predator(s) likely patrol these sections of highway, as they are the best sections for opportunity. Increased RCMP presence along these sections of Highway 16 will greatly reduce the number of potential targets, see recommendation #2, and will visually discourage the predator(s).

Recommendation #4—That the Greyhound Bus Company's "free ride" program be expanded, and target marketed to the population in the Highway 16 corridor who fit the victim profile. The Greyhound Bus Line is the only publicly available highway transportation system that delivers service along the entire length of the Highway of Tears. This company has a "free ride" program for individuals that cannot afford to pay for their rides, and it is a program that is not widely known to the public. This "free ride" program can be expanded for, and marketed specifically at, all young women who live along the Highway 16 corridor. Moreover, Greyhound Bus drivers who drive the Prince George to Prince Rupert route must be instructed to stop and pick up any hitchhiker who falls within the victim profile.

In reality, Greyhound never offered free rides to those who couldn't afford to pay.[21]

Nevertheless, the symposium recommendations certainly point out the significance that lack of transportation played in the crimes. In fact, Wally Oppal, Q.C, the commissioner of the 2010 Missing Women Commission of Inquiry, received many proposals about protecting Aboriginal and rural women. Echoing the Tears Symposium recommendations, he concluded that enhanced, safe public transportation was key.[22] But by early 2014, there was still no shuttle-bus service along the Highway of Tears. Not only that, but New Democratic Party MLA Jenny Kwan noted in the BC Legislature that there was still no budget or timeline for such a shuttle service.[23] Although BC Justice Minister Susan Anton said the government was working on the transportation issue in northern communities, NDP leader Adrian Dix described the issue as critical, considering especially that it had been identified eight years earlier.[24]

> Recommendation #5—That every public sector employee working between Prince George and Prince Rupert be contacted and used as a female-hitchhiker detection network. These public sector employees travel the Highway 16 corridor extensively and at all hours of the day and night. Coordination with these public sector employees, to detect and communicate the locations of women hitchhikers using their cell phones, would greatly assist the collective community in its victim-prevention efforts.

> Recommendation #6—That a number of "safe homes" similar to, and possibly including MCFD (Ministry of Children and Family Development, BC) and Aboriginal Social Service safe homes be established at strategic locations

along the entire length of Highway 16, between the cities of Prince Rupert and Prince George. In the event that young women are walking, or are picked up hitchhiking, in the evening or late at night, a safe place to spend the night will be necessary. A network of at least twenty-two safe homes, preferably within visual range of the highway, needs to be established between Prince Rupert and Prince George. These "safe homes" can also be used as hitchhiker check-in points ...

Recommendation #7—That the Rural Crime Watch Program be expanded to include a Highway Watch component along the full length of the Highway of Tears. In partnership with Regional Districts, Rural Community Associations and First Nations communities, residents of all houses located within visual range of Highway 16, between Prince George and Prince Rupert, need to be canvassed for support, and provided with a 1-800 crisis-line number in the event they see a young woman hitchhiking on the highway. Furthermore, that they be requested to watch the hitchhiker, and note the description of any vehicle who would stop and pick her up.

Recommendation #8—That a number of emergency phone booths be placed along the Highway at strategic locations between the cities of Prince Rupert and Prince George, British Columbia. The distance between the towns, cities, and First Nations communities exceeds 100 kilometres in some places along this highway. There are many stretches of the highway where cellular phones are out of transmission range. Should a potential victim's car break down, or a hitchhiker be seen getting into a vehicle, or car accident be witnessed, it is vital that motorists, and hitchhikers themselves, have closer access to a form of emergency communication. Telus Mobility should be approached to look into the feasibility of increasing cellphone coverage along the entire length of the highway, thus minimizing, or eliminating, no-signal areas.

Recommendation #9—That a number of billboards, and many more posters, be placed at strategic locations along the Highway 16 corridor between Prince George and Prince Rupert, British Columbia. These carefully designed billboards will be used to generate travelling public awareness on the issue of the murdered and missing women, and also contain a 1-800 number for the public to call in tips, potential leads, or even cell-phone call-in the location of any female hitchhiker they encounter. These billboards will also be viewed by hitchhikers and young women, and thus should also be considered part of a victim-prevention campaign. The posters, distributed and posted at every gas station, restaurant, business, and community service centre, located along the entire length of the Highway of Tears, will accomplish the same objectives as the strategically placed billboards.

Unfortunately, bureaucracy got involved and soon after, the wording of the signs became an issue, so the small number of these that were eventually erected along the highway were extremely slow coming.[25]

Recommendation #10—That an annual awareness and prevention campaign be delivered to every elementary school, high school, college, university, and silviculture company located in, and between, the cities of Prince Rupert and Prince George prior to the hitchhiking and tree-planting season. Primarily the hitchhiking and tree-planting seasons coincide, more specifically both commence, in the spring. Many of the young Aboriginal women who disappeared were hitchhiking during the summer months, and at least three of them were younger than seventeen years old; this means they were of high-school-student age. April is the month that denotes the end of college and university studies. There is always a mass spring migration, of primarily college and university students, from all areas of Canada, to the Highway 16 corridor for employment as tree planters. Nicole Hoar was one such individual. Therefore all silviculture companies operating in Central and North Coast British Columbia, should be required to provide Highway of Tears awareness as part of W.C.B (Workers' Compensation Board) mandated health and safety training for their employees.

The twenty-three other recommendations include, among other things: further awareness and prevention programs be delivered to every school, college and university educating people to the hazards of hitchhiking; organizing and the need for those in positions of power in all levels of government to listen to Aboriginal youth; the creation of recreation and social programs; related media campaigns; the increase in social services; the development of an emergency-readiness plan complete with readiness teams; the involvement of search-and-rescue and fire departments; the creation of a regional

First Nations crisis-response plan and team; fully qualified Aboriginal mental health therapists, grief counselors and other similar support workers; a First Nations advocate, board of directors and governing body; and a Highway of Tears Legacy Fund and two coordinators.

The report recommended the RCMP, who were mentioned forty-one times, "re-establish and maintain communication with each of the victims' families," and work to "bridge the communications and awareness gap that historically exists between them and First Nations communities along the Tears."

Although Solicitor General John Les, and North District's RCMP Chief Superintendent Barry Clark, the officer in charge of RCMP E-Division Northern Region and all communities along Highway 16 West of Prince George, expressed confidence that the recommendations could be realized,[26] many in the public arena quickly recognized that some were unrealistic and unachievable. In fact, one northern newspaper reporter suggested that the realization of many of the report's recommendations would be "tantamount to curing poverty and racism in northern BC."[27]

———

Lisa Krebs was the first Tears coordinator chosen after the Highway of Tears Symposium recommendations. She was hired in the fall of

2006 by Carrier Sekani Family Services and financed by the Solicitor General and Ministry of Children and Families.[28] Ms. Krebs had an impressive background in planning and a Bachelor's in First Nations Studies from the University of Northern British Columbia. She also had a Master of Anthropology degree from the University of Alberta.

One year into her contract Krebs acknowledged publicly that the only *Highway of Tears Symposium Report* recommendation that had been completed was the hiring of Ms. Krebs as a fulltime coordinator.[29] Shortly thereafter, funding for the coordinator's position ran out, and Ms. Krebs left with little fanfare. I heard from a very reliable source in Prince George that before leaving, Ms. Krebs provided her employer with a final report. If so, that report has never been released to the public, and my Access to Information Request of July 18, 2011 to the Carrier Sekani Family Services Privacy Coordinator in Prince George has never been acknowledged.

In 2009, Mavis Erickson, a former Carrier Sekani Chief, Harvard law graduate and the 1999 special representative to the Federal Minister of Indian Affairs, was named the second Highway of Tears coordinator. She immediately called a public inquiry into the Highway of Tears.[30] By May 2010, with unresolved funding issues, the coordinator called for another advocate, in addition to herself, to be located at the western end of the Highway of Tears.[31] To date, this position has not been created and despite all the study, action and perhaps inaction, it remains unclear what or how many of the recommendations have been realized or even how many have been addressed.

In October 2014, Wendy Kellas, manager of the Highway of Tears Initiative at Carrier Sekani Family Services, was saluted for among other things, "leading the creation" of the website www.highwayoftears.ca.[32] The website was made possible through funding from the Civil Forfeiture Office in partnership with Victim Services and Crime Prevention Division, Ministry of Justice. It acknowledges Carrier Sekani Family Services' commitment to "fulfilling the 33 recommendations from the *Highway of Tears Symposium Recommendation Report*,"[33] but fails to mention how many recommendations have been successfully implemented to date.

Implementation issues aside for the moment, Todd Hamilton, editor of the Smithers *Interior News*, pointed out something that was missing from the *Highway of Tears Recommendation Report*, something that was obvious to everyone living along Highway 16. He wrote that there weren't enough police along the highway to handle the number of complaints that were flooding in from the Highway 16 communities. He questioned where the money was going to come from to increase the necessary policing, suggesting that just tossing money at victim assistance, adding a couple new telephones or bus services "isn't going to stop the carnage on the Highway of Tears."[34]

7. ViCLAS—THE RCMP'S COMPUTER CYBER SLEUTH

"Unlike a police officer, ViCLAS (Violent Crime Linkage System) does not retire, does not miss work, does not move to a new jurisdiction. ViCLAS never forgets the nitty-gritty of the case and it's always there to compare."—Inspector Ron MacKay (RCMP, retired)[1]

Occasionally I conduct an adult-education course called Introduction to Private Investigation. One section of the course focuses on observation and the ability to listen, which is different from the ability to hear. If you cannot effectively listen, messages are often misunderstood. Also, we listen to our mind's never-ending chatter after we observe an event or read something important. To demonstrate this, I either privately tell one student, or give them a card to read which has a one- or two-sentence summary of critical events that form part of a fictional crime. Once that's done I ask that person to privately relate these facts to the next person in the row, who will do the same to the next in line and so on, until the last person at the back of the classroom has been told the story. This last person then relates it back to the class. It's a take on the broken-telephone classic.

A simple two-sentence summary of events might have started as: "Two people robbed the 7-11 store on Main Street. One was a twenty-five-year-old female with red hair and one was a sixteen-year-old boy with blond hair." You would be amazed at how screwed up these two sentences become by the time they are finally related by the last person in class.

Six months after the Tears Symposium—and six months after the RCMP announced it would be conducting a major review of the Highway of Tears cases—Vancouver RCMP Communications Officer, Staff Sergeant John Ward, confirmed that eight investigators and data-entry people continued to enter Tears data into an unnamed computer program—the same way it had been done before the symposium. The entire process was described by Ward as "massive, detailed, and time-consuming."[2] It's important to know if this group of investigators was trained in data entry, and whether their "data-entry people," as described by the staff sergeant, were professionally qualified or whether, as rumoured, they were retirees and friends of the force.

Can you imagine what might happen if a group of semi- or unqualified data-entry personnel and supervisors began sifting through thousands of pieces of paper, attempting to decipher police investigators' handwritten notes and investigation reports from past crimes ranging in age from one to thirty years, then entering their versions of events into a police computer? Yes, something akin to a broken telephone. And common sense tells us that the margin of error in such a process would be staggering. According to PublicEngines, a provider of cloud-based solutions that facilitates crime analysis, recent audits show that "up to twenty-five percent of a typical agency's data is incorrect." In general, these errors occur at the point of data entry.[3] Perhaps the RCMP's failure to enter these cases into ViCLAS prior to the symposium was one reason why it took them six months to admit ViCLAS was being used.

The acronym ViCLAS stands for "Violent Crime Linkage System," an RCMP computer system capable of connecting a series of crimes that have been committed by the same person. In October 2006, in reference to the Highway of Tears investigation, Ward said: "When all the data is entered, investigators will have the capability to look for connections or other items of interest that may not be possible by a manual cross-referencing effort." He further noted that he wasn't "sure if the program has been used for other investigations," but that its "level of sophistication and ability to track information will help investigators."[4] A Harvard University professor and a consultant on the Federal Bureau of Investigation's "Violent Criminal Apprehension Program (ViCAP)" computer system, explained that Canadians had done to their ViCLAS computer system what the Japanese did to the assembly-line: they took a good American idea and transformed it into the best in the world.[5]

Given this information, and from a Tears investigative perspective, a lingering question remains: why did it take the RCMP until 2006 to begin entering murdered and missing women's case information into such a valuable asset as ViCLAS?

The RCMP said the process of creating ViCLAS started in Canada in the 1980s after it became apparent "that complex, multi-jurisdictional investigations, such as that of serial killer Clifford Olson in British Columbia, could benefit from a central repository capable of gathering, collating and comparing violent crimes." They also told us that ViCLAS came about after researching and " adopting the best features of the American models and then incorporating the latest behavioural research findings and current technology." In addition to a number of other crimes, unsolved homicides *and* missing persons cases are ("where the circumstances indicate a strong possibility of foul play and the victim is still missing") *all* potential ViCLAS cases.[6]

Unfortunately for the Highway of Tears cases, the true implementation date of ViCLAS across the country is shrouded in contradiction. RCMP Fact Sheets from 2000 and 2001 show that ViCLAS was born in 1991. Initially, each ViCLAS unit across the country had its own provincial database, which by 2000-01 were all linked together.[7] One outside source agrees 1991 is the date ViCLAS was unveiled in Canada,[8] however the 2007 version of the RCMP's website on the subject contradicts both sources by citing the implementation date as 1994.[9] Yet another RCMP source pegged the start date of ViCLAS in British Columbia as 1992.[10] This was contradicted by yet another RCMP source, a 2007 issue of the

RCMP *Gazette,* which states the program was developed in 1995.[11] To complicate or simplify matters, depending on which way you look at it, the 2011, 2013 and 2014 versions of the RCMP's website completely omit the ViCLAS implementation date altogether.[12]

Whatever the case, it seems safe to assume that ViCLAS was first available for use by the RCMP in BC sometime between 1992 and 1995. The ViCLAS start date is crucial here because Ramona Wilson, Roxanne Thiara and Leah Alishia Germaine were all murdered in 1994. Lana Derrick went missing in 1995, Nicole Hoar disappeared in 2002 and Tamara Chipman disappeared in 2005. The victims' families and general public deserve to know how many of these cases were not entered into ViCLAS until 2006 and, if there was a significant delay, why did it take the RCMP so long to make use of a computer program that they not only had available for use in BC, but have successfully sold internationally to Belgium, Czech Republic, France, Germany, Ireland, Netherlands, New Zealand, Switzerland, and the UK.[13]

Sergeant Chris Wozney, a Mountie who worked with ViCLAS in Vancouver, believes that "(p)olicemen are very traditional in their attitudes" and that "(w)e're slow to admit there might be a new and better way." Wozney also said investigators don't believe in ViCLAS, an attitude she described that was "ego" related. They feel, she furthered, that *"I can solve my case without your help, thank you."*

A year later those claims appeared to ring true when it was learned that BC police officers reported that fewer than thirty percent of all relevant cases were entered into ViCLAS, and across Canada, the RCMP had more than 2,000 cases waiting to be entered into ViCLAS along with another 7,000 in queue to be ViCLAS analyzed.[15]

There was even an acknowledgement on the RCMP's website as late as 2007 that noted that ViCLAS was still not being used to its full potential: "Many investigators are resistant to investing the time and effort it takes to complete the (ViCLAS) booklet. Most, as you might expect, would rather be out knocking on doors or making arrests."[16]

It's unclear whether the RCMP overcame the ViCLAS problem of "investigator resistance," but a check of the RCMP website in the fall of 2011 revealed that it no longer makes any reference to ViCLAS whatsoever. If there is one thing I've learned from being an RCMP "armchair quarterback," it's what's *not* said that's often as important as what *is* said.

Issues such as investigator resistance, of compliance, and the fact that the use of ViCLAS is legally mandated in only two Canadian provinces are even more disturbing when we look at the bigger picture. Canadian police forces admit there is a significant number of serial offenders committing crimes against people. By 2010 the Native Women's Association of Canada identified 582 missing and murdered Indigenous women and girls across the country. In 2014 the RCMP identified a total of 1,181 murdered and missing Aboriginal women's cases in Canada.[17] These facts do not appear to compel Canadian police investigators to enter all qualifying cases on ViCLAS, as evidenced by the RCMP assertion that the numbers would "increase dramatically" if investigators were compelled to put such cases on ViCLAS,[18] nor does it appear to compel lawmakers who are aware of this problem to legislate police forces across Canada to use the ViCLAS system.

In 1999 BC Attorney General Ujjal Dosanjh said he was drafting a resolution which would force BC's police chiefs to plug the gaping holes in law enforcement's computer system for tracking serial killers and rapists. His decision was based on the failed promise made the previous year by the BC Association of Chiefs of Police that one hundred percent of all relevant cases would be filed and entered on ViCLAS beginning January 1999. In May 1999 the *Vancouver Sun* reported that the RCMP statistics obtained by the paper showed that in the first three months of 1999, police officers across the province failed to submit ViCLAS reports on more than sixty percent of homicides, sexual assaults, abductions and other crimes.[19]

In 2001, Abbotsford Police Inspector Rod Gehl told the *Vancouver Sun* that many homicide cases in most jurisdictions are still kept on index cards and hard copies, not on computer systems, thereby creating a real lack of information available for sharing. Staff Sergeant Doug Bruce, head of the West Vancouver Police Major Crimes Unit, said ViCLAS is a useful tool, but there would be a vast improvement in the justice system if the province could also adopt a centralized computer system. He said that while British Columbia police forces currently rely on ViCLAS, they also rely on personal communication, and in some cases, media reports, to spot links in cases. When ViCLAS does notify a police force that one of its files is similar to another police force's file, there are no guidelines to ensure that agencies follow up on the information or join forces and immediately go to work together. Corporal Pete Cross, a senior investigator in the Surrey RCMP Homicide Unit, told *Vancouver Sun* reporters that the lack of resources and a "paper" tip-filing system at his detachment was "still in the dark ages."[21]

In September 2010, the Missing Women Working Group, which was established in 2006 in response to the alarming number of murdered and missing women in Canada, released the report *Issues Related to the High Number of Murdered and Missing Women in Canada*. It recommended that trained specialists be available to provide ViCLAS analysis to investigators; police investigators who receive a "potential linkage" report from ViCLAS should follow up with additional investigation in a timely manner; and police investigators and forensic lab personnel, upon receiving notification that a DNA linkage has been made on an outstanding case, should advise ViCLAS so that its personnel can update their database.[22]

In February 2012, the Missing Women Inquiry heard testimony from Mounties that in January 2001, ViCLAS case submission compliance with regards to police departments throughout the province, including the RCMP, was so bad there was no way to understand the scope and number of missing women. In an attempt to remedy this problem there was a ten-person team working on ViCLAS throughout Lower Mainland municipalities.[23] Although this admission of poor compliance was specific to the Lower Mainland, it is indicative of a more widespread problem and would most certainly have been a problem in Northern British Columbia and in all probability, the rest of Canada.

The sworn testimony of RCMP Deputy Commissioner of the Pacific Region, Gary Bass, given at the Missing Women Inquiry in May 2012, indicated that in the early 1990s he had identified a serious deficiency in the investigation of homicides, and it was highly suspected by some that there may be a serial killer operating on Vancouver Island, in the Fraser Valley, and in Northern British Columbia. At that time he also pegged the number of missing persons in the province at 1,800, many of which he said were women. Yet when asked about the former testimony of another

RCMP officer who had indicated that a lack of information had been identified, collected and entered into ViCLAS, Bass said he didn't know if he would agree with that officer. However, Bass described the person as a very competent police officer and profiler responsible for setting up and establishing ViCLAS.

Had senior Mounties in BC, as well as their RCMP counterparts throughout the country, insisted that all of their investigators invest the time and effort necessary to complete the ViCLAS booklet so their information could be entered into ViCLAS when it was fresh in their minds, perhaps certain realities would be different today. Instead, information was left for years, to be pulled from dusty file boxes and put into the database from old notes and reports, by investigators and data entry clerks who had nothing to do with the original investigations. Had this not been the reality, no one would be asking why it took until 2006 for the RCMP to enter cases into a computer program which was available sometime between 1991-1995. This way they could have started an electronic case-by-case comparative review in British Columbia and other jurisdictions so they could start seeing things with a "fresh set of electronic eyes."[24]

The victim's families and the public need to know why the RCMP conducted its second of two major file reviews of the Highway of Tears investigations in 2004 by cross-referencing information by hand.[25] They failed to make use of ViCLAS or any other program until early 2006 which would have otherwise allowed officers to easily compare cases.[26]

All this raises one significant question, along the Highway of Tears and perhaps across Canada, where the use of ViCLAS is not mandated by law. Unfortunately it's a question which nobody will ever be able to answer. That is, how many of these murdered and missing Aboriginal women would still be around today if ViCLAS was used in a timely manner?

The Canadian public should also be asking why senior members of the RCMP tasked with investigating Canada's most heinous and horrific crimes do not ensure that ViCLAS is used one hundred percent of the time in all cases of missing and murdered Aboriginal women. This is especially disturbing when there was solid evidence that the ViCLAS program works. For example, an RCMP case study shows that in BC in June 1992, while walking home from school, a fifteen-year-old girl was attacked and repeatedly assaulted. Investigators received hundreds of tips, yet after using huge amounts of police resources they failed to identify a suspect, even though he had not covered his face during the attack and the police were able to produce composite drawings. Three months later they submitted their information for inclusion into ViCLAS. Within one hour after inputting the data, a suspect who lived 800 kilometres north was identified. The man was arrested, confessed, convicted and sentenced to eight years in jail.[27]

Outside Canada, ViCLAS was implemented in the United Kingdom in 1998 and within a short eighteen-month period the computer program was given credit for linking an offence in Grampian, Scotland to the unsolved 1968 murder of a fourteen-year-old boy in Surrey, England.[28] The Canadian computer program also received credit for helping police solve the UK's "trophy rapist" case in which seven victims, one a ten-year-old child, were attacked and raped between 2001 and 2003. In this case ViCLAS was also credited with an estimated investigative-cost savings of two million pounds,[29] or approximately $4,575,000 Canadian.[30]

In response to a July 2011 Access to Information Act request, the RCMP advised that with the exception of Ontario and Quebec, no territories or provinces have legislation that makes submitting information to ViCLAS a legal requirement, although as per the RCMP's *Operations Manual* Policy OM.36.1.4, all ViCLAS cases must be reported to the division ViCLAS coordinator within thirty days of the investigation launch.

In such a light, the public should also be asking why our federal and provincial governments are failing to create legislation making submission of investigative information to ViCLAS a legal requirement in all murdered and missing women's cases.

8. LESSER OF TWO EVILS

"When you think there could be nine killers running around out there, a serial killer seems to me to be the lesser of two evils."
— Dan George, Chair of the Highway of Tears Symposium

Having never personally met Leland Switzer was a great disappointment. Leland was a man many, including quite a few members of the RCMP, loved to hate. He was convicted of second-degree murder for the June 23, 2002 shooting death of his brother Irwin on their Prince George family farm, and was sentenced to life in prison with no eligibility for parole for ten years.

The shooting took place two days after Nicole Hoar went missing. In late 2009 the Mounties very publicly dug up the yard of a rural property in Isle Pierre which had once been owned by Leland Switzer. Their actions and a lack of explanation for them have fuelled speculation along Highway 16 that continues today: that Leland was not only responsible for Nicole Hoar's disappearance, but that he is the Highway of Tears serial killer. I now disagree with the speculation, as did at least one RCMP staff sergeant I know.

My practical working theory had to include the possibility of a serial killer. I couldn't envision that these crimes were the work of a multitude of individual killers. Once I gathered what I thought was most of the available information, I started the investigative process. Only then did I begin to develop a working theory, which was influenced by the RCMP's understanding that there are a large number of serial offenders committing crimes against people on a regular basis. The Mounties describe ninety percent of all serial killers as psychopaths. Some psychopathic traits are identified as "deviant arousal; low impulse control; and previous violence."[1] Unfortunately, it was not inconceivable that one of these individuals might be operating along the Highway of Tears. Or was the Highway of Tears tragedy the work of nine or more individual killers? The chair of the 2006 Highway of Tears Symposium told a Prince George newspaper: "When you think there could be nine killers running around out there, a serial killer seems to be the lesser of two evils."[2] In fact, Nicole Hoar's father Jack was convinced there was a serial killer working the area. If there wasn't, he felt "there would be a bunch of different people killing a whole bunch of different people, creating a much bigger issue for the RCMP."[3]

Although the RCMP wasn't talking publicly about the possibility of a serial killer travelling the Highway of Tears, in March of 2006 BC's solicitor general John Les was. He seemed to think some of the killings showed signs that a serial killer was at work. After the solicitor general's remarks, the RCMP wavered, suggesting they couldn't rule out the possibility of a serial killer but thought for some reason the idea "smacks of sensationalism."[4] More "smoke and mirrors," when you consider the fact that, as previously mentioned, the RCMP suspected there was a serial killer.[5] Later in March, John Les flip-flopped, saying there did not appear to be much evidence to support a serial-killer theory and that's why the police had not formed a task force to investigate. Then just one month later, another flip-flop. This time Les said there was a fifteen-member targeted team of police officers working eight investigations into murdered and missing women dating back to 1990.[6]

In its 2008 report, *Serial Murder: Multi-Disciplinary Perspectives for Investigators*, the FBI claim serial killers choose their victims based on availability or the victim's lifestyle. They also choose their victims based on vulnerability, how personally appealing they are with regards to considerations of gender, race and ethnic background, age, or any number of specific preferences of the killer.[7] This selection process could have easily been used in the cases of several of the Tears victims whose traits and circumstances were similar.

My investigative strategy always begins with an original working theory. However, it is a "work in progress" rather than something carved in stone. The theory evolves each time new information reveals that some part of the original theory was either correct, incorrect, or in need of modification. Using this approach, I almost always achieve what I originally set out to accomplish: to find the truth. There was no reason this approach wouldn't work on the Highway of Tears cases. To find the truth, my investigative methods would include what were once described by the Mounties' Major Crime Unit boss Leon Van De Walle as "investigator's skill and intuition."[8] This process included gathering information, gossip and rumours and then following up on that information by knocking on doors and getting in people's faces looking for answers.

I began gathering information by talking to whoever would talk to me. As a private investigator, my philosophy has always been that I need all the help I can get, and I'm willing to accept it from whoever will give it to me. There are no boundaries, and I don't arbitrarily turn away from, look down on, or treat anyone with contempt or indignity. It was inevitable that some of my information would come from criminals, some currently active and others incarcerated, ex-convicts, bikers and wannabe bikers, prostitutes, drug dealers, and homeless people. The truth is their information is often more valuable than the information one might get from a shop owner, schoolteacher or businessperson. I knew that in order to get their cooperation and the information I needed, these people had to be treated with the same respect you would give more mainstream members of society, no matter how distasteful their backgrounds. If I did otherwise, they would disrespect and shun me in the same way they disrespect and avoid the police. No one knew who the hell I was, I wasn't a cop, I didn't live anywhere around the Highway of Tears, I wasn't Native, or a member of any victim's family—and I wasn't on anyone's payroll. Sure, they might think I'm weird and suspicious. But I was compelled.

Once I gathered most of the available information I needed to get started, I headed out on the road and door by door, determined to prove or disprove my theory. While forensic or crime-scene evidence could be crucial to obtaining a conviction, that evidence, if available, had already been gathered and processed by the police. For the most part, I wouldn't be looking for forensic evidence. I don't believe in cookie-cutter-style investigations, so there are no hard-and-fast rules. However, one exception might involve gathering forensic evidence in the form of a suspect's DNA in the hope the RCMP had DNA from the crime scene on file, and a comparison could then be done. I envisioned this process taking place without the suspect's knowledge because it would be foolish to expect cooperation.

Before I ever attempted this, I had to very seriously consider the question of how far I could legally go to obtain DNA. And if successful, what would I do next to get the RCMP's cooperation? I tackled the easiest problems first by researching the DNA aspect of my investigation. In 2000, the Court of Appeal for Saskatchewan ruled a lower court had not erred when it issued a warrant to an RCMP officer who partially relied on the work of private investigators. A PI may well have violated the law in gathering the sample of material from which a DNA profile was obtained. But the

Court of Appeal also ruled that private investigators cannot be said to be agents of the state. For this reason, a PI's actions in gathering samples of material could not be found to be in violation of constitutional rights, even if a sample was collected illegally.[9]

This provided me with the legal parameters for my DNA search. If I was fortunate enough to obtain DNA, I would send it to a private lab for analysis. Next I would forward the private lab's results to the RCMP for comparison to any DNA samples on file. This strategy, rather than just forwarding the DNA directly to the RCMP, would make it harder for them to ignore it. My research led me to the Lakehead University Paleo-DNA Laboratory, in Thunder Bay, Ontario. The lab has been working on cold casework for national law enforcement organizations and has been profiling hair samples for the RCMP and provincial police.[10] They went out of their way to help and were very accommodating in answering my questions and sending me down the correct path to obtaining a good, workable sample.

Based on a serial-killer theory I was drawn to three cases. There is an old real-estate adage investors and buyers rely on when purchasing property: "Location, location, location." This can also help when comparing similar crimes—police experts refer to it as "geographic profiling." Comparing Tears cases and using a little investigator intuition, I began to look at the murder of Roxanne Thiara and Leah Alishia Germaine in 1994 and the disappearance of Nicole Hoar in

2002. Roxanne and Leah were friends and all three girls were last seen on a Friday. I had previously spent quite a bit of time in Prince George working on various other investigations and had become familiar with the city. Although Roxanne's body was found on the outskirts of Burns Lake, a three-hour drive west of Prince George, Leah's body was found behind Leslie Road school in southeast Prince George. This location was just off Highway 16, a very short distance from the highway where Nicole Hoar was last seen.

It seemed unlikely to me that Leah's murderer would have been driving around an unknown rural residential community searching for a dumpsite for her body. My theory was her killer or killers would have known the area before dumping her body at the school. She wasn't left there by coincidence. I continue to believe that this location is somehow significant to her killer. Highway 16 is a lonely, remote stretch of highway with thousands of much better places to stash a body than a well-populated community with many potential witnesses. Whoever killed Leah Germaine may have been trying to send a message to others attempting to escape Prince George's sex trade industry and needed her body found. To choose this specific location they may have either lived in the area, lived there previously or knew someone, perhaps a friend or relative, they had visited there.

My theory also included the possibility that Leah's killer may have been returning to or had been leaving the same area eight years later, on Friday, June 21, 2002. As such, he could also be responsible for Nicole Hoar's disappearance; she was last seen in this area, at the Mohawk gas station at Highway 16 and Gauthier Road. I also had to ask myself if it was just a coincidence Roxanne and Leah were friends and both had been murdered on a Friday.

Armed with my first working theory, I found myself sitting in front of my computer hours before sunrise with what little hair I had left looking very Kramerish. I was trying to determine who owned property in the Leslie Road school area in 1994 and find out if they still owned the same property. If not, did they still live along the Highway of Tears? Once I had a list of names I would then be able to research what, if any, criminal charges these people faced in the past.

In addition to computer analysis, I would also rely on help from Telus. Prior to BC Tel's merger with Telus, they maintained a library of old telephone directories in their corporate office in Burnaby. Their library directories dated back to the very first telephone directory BC Tel published. During a couple of previous unrelated investigations I had easily been able to make appointments with BC Tel to view the books. Unfortunately, this time I was politely brushed off by a Telus representative and told to contact Yellow Pages. A ridiculous request considering Yellow Pages is not a residential-listing service. Nonetheless, I called Yellow Pages who said they did not have copies of Telus White Pages directories and referred me back to Telus. My last hope then was to contact local libraries in towns along the Highway of Tears, in the hope they kept copies of old telephone directories. Some did and others didn't. This made the entire investigative process very time-consuming. It soon proved to be a massive undertaking which could result in a list of hundreds and hundreds of names, making it virtually impossible for me to completely follow up on. I needed a new approach, which I began by mailing hundreds of flyers to the people currently living in my target area. The flyer had pictures of Leah Germaine and Nicole Hoar, information about their cases, and a map of the area. On it I asked for anyone with any information, regardless of how insignificant it might seem, to contact me. I never received one call so I put that approach on the backburner, at least for the time being, and in early 2006 I refocused my attention elsewhere.

My research regarding the circumstances surrounding the 1994 murder of Roxanne Thiara didn't reveal much that I could go on. So I started to look again. In a note posted on the original Highway of Tears website, someone who identified only by the initials "N.J." from Quesnel, British Columbia, described Roxanne as having been the best friend of one of her foster daughters. She also described her as a beautiful, lively girl but very sad who once referred to herself as "no good." The writer explained: "Even after attempts were made to assure her that making mistakes doesn't make anyone 'no good,' she didn't believe it."

Similar to Roxanne's case, information regarding Leah Germaine's life and subsequent murder was scarce. While some described Leah as a drug user who sometimes turned to prostitution,[11] someone else described her as "so full of life, always smiling with that big pie face," a reference to a nickname she didn't like. Leah was also described as "a very strong-willed, stubborn little girl with a mind of her own but oh so sweet inside."[12] An anonymous plea was also posted on the Highway of Tears website: "To the friends of Leah who knew her on the streets of Prince George ... we are still waiting and praying you will come forward even after all these years. You all know who did this to her and Roxanne (Leah's friend) ... just recently, one of you has come forward to the RCMP in Prince George but we need more witnesses to this case. Please ... if you have any kind of conscience help us take this wacko killer off the streets of P.G."

One of the problems with my serial-killer theory involved the length of time between crimes. While Leah and Roxanne were both murdered in 1994, Nicole Hoar didn't go missing until 2002, eight years later. But according to American professor of criminology Dr. Scott A. Bonn, serial killers experience an emotional cooling-off period between murders. During these times, the killer returns to "his/her seemingly normal life until the urge to kill becomes overwhelming." The duration of the cooling-off period can vary from weeks to months or even years, and varies by killer.[13] Incarceration for other unrelated crimes can also affect the timescale. Thus, I didn't think an eight-year period between crimes was argument enough to disprove my first serial-killer theory.

———

My interest in Leland Switzer began in 2006 not long after he was tried in court for killing his brother Irwin. The accused testified that he fired a quick shot from a .308 rifle to prevent his brother from beating him. The fatal bullet struck his brother in the chest, near the heart. It was then I received a telephone call from an anonymous caller. The woman told me she had been flagging for a road crew somewhere along Highway 16. She said that while she had traffic stopped a biker told her that someone by the name of "Chug" killed Nicole. At the time I had no idea that Leland's nickname was Chug, so I did some research and managed to come up with the addresses for 107 individuals right across Canada with that surname. I sent everyone a letter asking if they or anyone they knew with the same surname had ever spent any time in Northern British Columbia, in particular around 2002.

Shortly after the letters were mailed, I received a telephone call from a sergeant who said he was in charge of a small-town RCMP detachment on Canada's East Coast. He was calling because an elderly gentleman in his community had received my letter. The man thought it was critical that his local police call to let me know that neither he nor his relatives had ever been in British Columbia. That call was the only response I received from this letter campaign.

In time my list of contacts grew and Leland Switzer came to my attention once again. I acquired a copy of the transcript of a voluntary statement he made to the RCMP on August 31, 2004, from a confidential source. The statement doesn't explain how Switzer's meeting with Sergeant Bruce Ward and Constable Karen Boreham was arranged, but it appears that Switzer called them. The conversation began with Leland producing an electronic gadget which he said he found wired in his wall, suggesting it was some kind of recording device. Sergeant Ward then explained that the Major Crime Unit tape-recorded all their conversations. Leland responded by telling him not to record the conversation and was unaware the Mounties were already secretly recording him.

The transcript shows that after leaving in a vehicle driven by Ward, the three stopped at a place that Leland identified as Nanoose Springs, formerly Baldy Hughes radar station. As they sat at some picnic tables, the still secretly taped conversation continued, but no one explained on tape where exactly this location was. My research places them thirteen kilometres southwest of Prince George. Baldy Hughes Air Force Station was operated by the United States Air

Force. It opened in June 1953 as part of the Pinetree Line of Ground-Control Intercept (GCI) radar sites. The station had been turned over to the RCAF in 1963 and closed in 1988. It is now home to the Baldy Hughes Addiction Treatment Centre.[14]

The discussion that followed amounted to sixty-eight transcribed pages of Leland's voluntary conversation with the two major-crime police investigators. The reason Leland met with police seems to be his desire to explain why he and a friend had stopped near the Mohawk gas station around the time Nicole Hoar disappeared. He said they had been drinking and stopped there, and then he "took a piss on the ground." He was worried the police might have his DNA, making him a suspect in Nicole's disappearance, so he wanted to explain why he was in the area where Nicole had last been seen.[15]

Leland and his brother Irwin were well-known characters in and around Prince George and also Isle Pierre, located some forty-five kilometers northwest of Prince George. I once described Isle Pierre to Robert Remington of the *Calgary Herald* as "bizarre," like "something out of *Deliverance*," a place with "snarling pit bulls and men who drive around at night on ATVs shooting rifles into the air."[16] As you travel north on Isle Pierre Road, you pass Canfor Forest Products' saw mill on your way to what's left of the old Isle Pierre townsite. The remnants of dilapidated buildings make it look like an old ghost town, but most of the homes are occupied by people. The only evidence of human existence being the satellite television dishes hanging precariously from the rotten wooden sidings, and the newer pickup trucks sprinkled among the old beaters and wrecks you'd expect.

When I was there the townsite and its inhabitants were guarded by a female pit bull. She was chained to a steel cable which was strung about five feet off the ground, running parallel to Isle Pierre Road. This allowed her to patrol the town's entrance back and forth along the length of the chain. A year later the only change in her life were the pups hanging off her teats as she stood guard. In the background were the sounds of more dogs, warning strangers who might want to enter uninvited.

Leland described himself to the Mounties as "different."[17] Based on what I've been told by friends and neighbours, I believe that was an understatement. The seasoned criminal had a local reputation for being a bit of a "Jekyll and Hyde" character. A number of people told me in confidence Leland flip-flopped between being a Christian, a heavy drug user, and a provider of security to marijuana grow-ops. At the time of his meeting with the RCMP, he was wearing a T-shirt with a logo he had designed when working at West Lake, the most sophisticated grow-op in Northern BC. Leland told police that only people who were part of the team were allowed to wear it.

Leland also seemed to have a compassionate side. On one

occasion, for instance, an elderly couple who Leland did odd jobs for, had their new television stolen. A short time after learning about the problem, Leland showed up at their home with their stolen television. Before he left, he gave them his personal assurance that neither their television or, for that matter, anything else they owned, would ever be stolen from their home again.

Leland's "good side," if you can call it that, revealed itself on another occasion, during a trip I took to Prince George in 2007. A woman telephoned me but would not identify herself by name. She said she was Leland's friend and asked me to meet her at a local coffee shop. When we met, she still refused to identify herself but told me she had known Leland for a long time and was insistent that he would never be involved with Nicole Hoar's disappearance or any of the Highway of Tears cases. She said he was the type of guy who went out of his way to help women. She explained that she had been abused at the hands of a man whom she and her family knew, but no one would do anything about it. So she confided in her longtime friend Leland Switzer. The woman said she didn't know what Leland said or did to her abuser, if anything, but she never saw the man or was bothered by him again.

There are several interesting snippets of information in Leland's taped conversation that shed light on his character. His father was of German descent, and though he only mentioned his mother once, he did refer to himself as Native, which suggests she may have been Aboriginal. Leland told investigators: "You know, I just got beat lots." He explained that when he was twelve his father would grab him by the arm and beat him with a sixteen-foot V-belt which had been cut in half. After one of those beatings, his father went out to his shop to work. Leland said he grabbed his rifle off the rack and walked out there, where his father watched him load the gun out of the corner of his eye. He then told him: "Dad, if you ever beat me like that again, I'm gonna kill ya." After that his father never hit him again.

During the interview Leland said that when people needed something collected, they got him to do it. His explanation: "God created man, Colonel Colt made them equal." He made several references to guns, saying: "Yeah, everybody thinks it's easy to just go whack somebody. Go fuckin' try it."

In reference to his children, he said that one time his kids were out in the river when three dogs approached. One was part wolf and part Rottweiler which attacked them. Leland fought the animal, killing it with his bare hands. When the dog's owner displayed anger, Leland demanded money for the pair of Vanier sunglasses he lost in the river during the struggle.

He also told investigators he had once been asked to assassinate someone outside Canada, describing himself as "a shooter." He went on to explain how he could shoot three bullets through a space the size of a quarter at 100 yards, using a rifle with iron sights, not a telescope. However, Leland said he declined the assassination job because "he was not God's executioner."

There were several gun-related stories about Leland I've heard over the years. One involves his wife, who during the summer would parade around Isle Pierre wearing only a bikini and stilettos in front of as many men as possible. No matter how often she walked by, and as much as they wanted too, no man would dare sneak a peek. They knew Leland as a marksman and rightfully feared that if caught, it would cost them.

Leland also had a somewhat violent relationship with the RCMP. At one time or another he faced a variety of charges, including failing to stop for police; resisting or obstructing police; uttering threats; mischief over $5,000; being unlawfully at large; and assault.[18] He also said "he liked getting out of the car to argue with the uniforms" and was known to tote a sawed-off shotgun in a duffel bag, telling suspected undercover police not to arrest him while in possession of the bag.

He further explained that at age sixteen he made a promise to his mother that he would not kill his brother.[19] At no time did Leland ever admit to the murder of his brother, nevertheless he liked to tell this story a lot, and it would eventually be one of the things that put him in prison.

Leland did though confirm rumours about a rave or benefit

dance held in the Blackwater area of Prince George around the time Nicole disappeared, and said he had attended it and had been seen by thirty-five people who knew him. He offered to take a lie-detector test with regards to her disappearance. However there is no record that the police ever asked him to take the polygraph at that time.

During Switzer's three-day murder trial, his lawyer attempted to convince BC Supreme Court Judge W. G. Parrett that Leland had shot his brother in self-defence. However, Judge Parrett said that Leland, as argued, did not fire a warning shot that went tragically wrong. Leland knew guns and clearly saw his brother advancing toward him. Leland was subsequently convicted of murder and unsuccessfully appealed the ruling in 2007.

———

In late August 2009, Bruce Hulan, a Vancouver RCMP staff sergeant, was so convinced that Switzer was a viable suspect in the Nicole Hoar case that a team of Mounties dug up his former yard in Isle Pierre. A multitude of police personnel set up tents and numerous pieces of earth-moving equipment. Two search-and-rescue dogs from Alberta, trained in the detection and recovery of human remains, examined the area, along with ground-penetrating radar operated by a geophysicist to detect anomalies in the earth.

As though making a conscious effort to rule out the possibility of a serial killer, an RCMP "E" Division communications officer said the search was for the remains of one person only. Then, to everyone's surprise and without warning, they packed up and left the area with no explanation other than there would be no disclosure as to what, if anything, they found on the search site.[20]

This unsuccessful search was the last bit of information given the public regarding Nicole Hoar's investigation until November 2013, when Elaine O'Connor, a reporter for *The Province* wrote that Leland Switzer agreed to take a polygraph. A private letter from Sergeant Bob Barrett of the RCMP's "E" Division to Leland Switzer had been released on social media. In it Sergeant Barrett stated that Leland had agreed to take the polygraph test regarding the Nicole Hoar murder and went on to explain: "If Leland passed the RCMP would release a letter to the media and parole board advising them of his cooperation and that the Mounties no longer consider him a person of interest in the Nicole Hoar investigation." RCMP Sergeant Peter Thiessen confirmed the letter was genuine but would not release the results of the polygraph. He did say though that to date "over 100 persons of interest have been polygraphed by Project E-PANA investigators."[21]

The RCMP later acknowledged giving Leland Switzer such a letter, and agreeing to release a message to the media and parole board advising them of his cooperation. The RCMP also acknowledged that they no longer consider Leland Switzer a person of interest in the Nicole Hoar investigation. However, they didn't provide that letter to the media after the polygraph examination. In light of this, I don't believe the RCMP lied to Leland in the letter.[22] I believe that he simply didn't pass the polygraph—but that doesn't necessarily mean he failed. My best guess is that Leland Switzer did not fail or pass; rather, his results were "inconclusive."

I find it interesting that in 1978, a BC court was the first in Canada to accept polygraph evidence, something the Supreme Court of Canada has since ruled inadmissible.[23] The RCMP believe: "When it comes to police work it is essential that investigators use all of the tools at their disposal to ensure they have accurate, reliable information. Forensic polygraph examinations are an integral part of their arsenal." They claim polygraph exams do not "detect lies but they do indicate when deceptive behaviour is being displayed," and "polygraph examinations don't replace in-depth investigations, they are an integral part of modern policing."[24] In 1996 Robert Russell, a former RCMP polygraph expert, agreed saying: "It's an aid to investigation," not "the be all and end all." Sheldon Pinx, the chairman of the national criminal justice section of the Canadian Bar Association, believes the polygraph is "not sufficiently sophisticated to the point where they [courts] would place credence in it," further arguing that the polygraph "doesn't, at the end of the day, say you're being truthful or dishonest. It simply provides certain information to polygraphists who are going to interpret those readings and come up with an opinion."[25] Perhaps that's why RCMP Deputy Commissioner Gary Bass told the Missing Women Commission of Inquiry, in reference to polygraphs, that "it wouldn't be uncommon for some investigators to refer to them having a Ouija board."[26]

As mentioned earlier, Leland Switzer described himself as "different." Maybe that's why he gave the parole board a letter indicating that he had passed the RCMP polygraph examination.[27] This letter, however, was not written on RCMP letterhead.

On many occasions I have tried to visit Leland Switzer in prison. But I've never received permission. As recently as January 2015 I sent him another letter in federal prison. The letter explained I was in the process of writing a book about the Highway of Tears which included him, and I requested visitation. I never received a reply. Either the warden involved the RCMP, who put an end to my plans, or, as in the past, he simply does not want to talk. This man may be a convicted murderer, but I am now in agreement with Prince George's Staff Sergeant Quinton Smith that Leland Switzer never had anything to do with Nicole Hoar's disappearance. I have no evidence to indicate his involvement or point me in that direction.

9. CRAZY WHITE MAN

"Those who have worn out their shoes many times know where to step."
— Chief Dan George

The area in Prince George formerly called the VLA, a neighbourhood originally built to accommodate soldiers home from the Second World War, is now known to locals as "The Hood." The Hood is home to gang members who do their business out of several crack houses, unafraid of using the hidden guns they often carry.[1] Staff Sergeant Brad Anderson summed up the RCMP's crime-reduction strategy for The Hood: getting chronic offenders clean; identifying and targeting prolific offenders and the locations they frequent; and sending them to jail. *The alternative?* Move them to someone else's jurisdiction. Anderson justified his approach by pointing out that his job was to do what it takes to protect Prince George.[2] His is a very practical, often forgotten, and today, unacceptable old-school approach to policing. That said, Roxanne Thiara and Leah Germaine would have been very familiar with The Hood.

I felt as strongly as ever that there was some merit to my original theory. Roxanne Thiara's November 1994 murder, the murder of Roxanne's friend Leah Germaine in December 1994, and the disappearance of Nicole Hoar in 2002 could very well be linked.

I first came to this conclusion while conducting an investigation for an insurance company in Prince George in the summer of 2006. During that investigation I found myself working in both The Hood and the Beaverly area of southwest Prince George where I unintentionally drove past the Haldi Road Elementary School on Leslie Road, the location where Leah Germaine's body was found. As I drove out of the area heading north, I realized that Nicole Hoar had last been seen at a location just a five-minute drive away. In other words, the general area where Leland Switzer's family had once lived, where he had murdered his brother, and where he had stopped to relieve himself—as he later made a point of telling police. My conclusion was later reinforced by information I received from the street. Information from people such as the addict who explained to uniformed Gang Task Force member Mark Jordan that he wouldn't want to owe a gang member hereabouts any money because "they'll cut your finger off for twenty dollars."[3]

If my theory was correct and all three or any combination were killed by the same individual, solving one case could result in solving the other. In my opinion, if there is a serial killer working the Highway of Tears he may be the only serial killer terrorizing women along that stretch of road.

Prior to 2002, very few people had ever heard the term "Highway of Tears."[4] That changed on Friday, June 21. Nicole Hoar, the eighth and only white Tears victim, was last seen hitchhiking near a gas station in Prince George as she attempted to make her way to Smithers to visit her sister. Her disappearance, unlike the previous murders and disappearances, was followed by a very high-profile police investigation. This police response, however, brought an old concern to the forefront. Years earlier, Matilda Wilson, the mother of 1995 murder victim Ramona Wilson, dared to ask: *Would my daughter's investigation have been handled differently had she been a blue-eyed blonde?* Many others were now asking the same type of question.

Nicole has been described by friends as confident, pleasant and outgoing with a great attitude and desire to learn. Her family described her as one capable of taking care of herself in the wilderness, as evidenced by a trip she once made to South America.[5] The twenty-five-year-old tree planter was employed by Celtic Restorations in Prince George. She was last seen by a coworker who dropped her off at the Mohawk gas station at Highway 16 and Gauthier Road so she could begin a trip to Smithers to meet her sister at a music festival. She was eventually reported missing July 2 after failing to return to her tree-planting job.

A week later after a massive four-day ground search failed to locate Nicole, the RCMP said they were planning to follow up on the 100-plus tips they had recently received. That said, Corporal Frank Henley of British Columbia's Historical Homicide Unit responsible for cold cases, said that in the past they did look at Highway 16 cases. Unfortunately, he lost four officers to the Pickton investigation. As a result, he concluded: "I know about these murders, some of the history, some of the suspects, but in terms of any active pursuit of them, it's not happening."[6] The search was called off. Even more startling was Corporal Henley's honest disclosure that, as far as the Mounties were concerned, they were no longer pursuing any Tears suspects.

Nevertheless, news of Nicole's case carried far, capturing media interest in Eastern Canada. An *Ottawa Citizen* headline read: "RCMP calls off search for missing tree planter: Mysterious disappearance of Nicole Hoar echoes cases of others who vanished in the area." As well, Nicole's father later said that although the RCMP took his daughter's investigation seriously, they didn't have the manpower to deal with the abundance of tips that came in. Although the tips were time-sensitive, the RCMP said: "It took over a year and a half to work through the file." At the same time, Prince George RCMP spokesman Gary Goodwin said the investigation was winding down, as only 60 out of 1,400 tips remained active. When confronted with the case of fifteen-year-old missing girl Elizabeth Smart, who had been kidnapped from her home in Salt Lake City, Utah in 2002 but had been found alive approximately twenty-eight kilometres from her home nine months later, Goodwin remarked: "Wow, wouldn't that be something if we got that lucky."[7]

Although Nicole's missing person case was no closer to being solved than any other Tears case, the relative interest police had shown in other cases would give rise to Aboriginal demands for change. Eventually, it played a role in prompting the 2006 Highway of Tears Symposium, which took place one month before the five-year anniversary of Nicole's disappearance.

———

At the start of my investigation, I figured my chance of finding information relevant to the Tears cases was a long shot at best. As such, I didn't want to give any of the victims' families false hope. As a precaution, I made it my personal policy not to call them or involve them directly in my investigation. But this changed in 2006 after I placed a small card-sized notice in the *Terrace Standard* asking the public for help. I soon received a telephone call from a woman living on the outskirts of Terrace. She told me she had been walking in a heavily bushed area along the banks of the Skeena River, east of Terrace, where she found a tree-planter's shovel. The shovel, which had been propped up against a tree, was clearly out of place in the old-forest undergrowth. She knew Nicole was a tree planter and tree planters' shovels are very personal items. The woman wondered if I knew whether Nicole had her shovel with her the day she went missing. The woman speculated that if she didn't, the shovel she had found along the riverbank could be hers.

A tree planter's shovel is a much smaller, stronger version of the garden spade. It often weighs less than three pounds and is approximately three feet long, with the handle accounting for slightly more than two-thirds of its total length. The blade is about nine inches long and four to five inches wide. It has kick plates or "kickers," as planters refer to them, on each side of the handle, for use by the right or left foot. Today, the majority of tree planters are students working their way through university and have been described as "creative, zany, independent thinkers, who care about their health and their environment."[8] Like many golfers who choose particular brands of golf clubs or have them custom built to suit their swing, experienced planters often choose their shovel type, customizing it later to suit their planting style.

When I asked the caller if she had contacted Terrace RCMP, she said she had several times. She complained that each time she was brushed off by the person on the other end of the phone. As a result, she never got to tell a real cop about her find. Although it was early in my investigation, this still didn't surprise me. I had already heard several similar stories about what tipsters described as a lack of interest from the RCMP. For example, at one point during their investigation the RCMP had publicly announced they were looking for an orange-coloured car in relation to Nicole's disappearance. Two people, one an ex-corrections officer and the other a newspaper reporter, had each told me they had alerted police about the probability of seeing the car in question. The former corrections officer called the RCMP after having seen a car fitting the description parked on the street in downtown Terrace, but was told Nicole Hoar's case was not theirs. It was Prince George's, so the tipster was given a long-distance number and told to call there. The man said he called Prince George RCMP and left a message on the answering machine, but never heard back. The newspaper reporter also told me she had made a similar call to Smithers RCMP about the suspicious vehicle, and like the Terrace man, never heard back.

On my first trip to Terrace I met the woman with the shovel at her home. She was right, it was a tree planters' shovel, so I took a photograph and telephoned Nicole's dad, Jack Hoar. Jack told me Nicole's shovel, unlike the one found by the woman, had been customized. Nicole had done that by cutting down one of the kick plates, but more important was the fact that she did not have her shovel with her when she disappeared, rendering this possible clue invalid and therefore of no value to my investigation.

At some point early on in my Tears investigation I was contacted by Tamara Chipman's aunt, Gladys Radek. She was one of the organizers of the annual Walk for Justice, a champion of murdered and missing Aboriginal women's cases, and an outspoken advocate for the families of Tears victims. You couldn't miss Gladys as she drove around in her old 1998 GMC Safari cargo van she called "The War Pony," because, as she explained, "we were at war with the federal government demanding a public inquiry" into the murdered and missing cases. The War Pony was covered with photographs of more than 120 women neatly duct-taped to its sides.[9]

In 2006, Gladys invited me to meet at her Vancouver home so she could pass along some information she thought might be relevant to my investigation. In anticipation of my arrival, she told me to park out front and walk down the lane to the gate in the back fence. She made sure I understood that once there, I was not to enter the yard until I telephoned her. She said this was necessary because she had a rather large and unfriendly dog.

The first thing I heard when I arrived was the barking. I phoned Gladys who told me she would be right out after she put her leg on. (Put her leg on! I didn't know she wore a prosthetic leg.) As I slowly opened the gate, my eyes searching for her dog, I looked up four or five feet to the deck where Gladys was standing. The dog was by her side, looking down at me. It was the scruffiest, meanest big dog I'd seen in a long time. Because I was concentrating on the dog, it took a few seconds before I noticed Gladys was wearing a black T-shirt that had the words "Crazy Indian" painted across the front in silver glitter. As I made my way up the stairs to the deck, I thought my black shirt should have sported the words, "Crazy White Man."

By the time I got up the steps to the deck she was already inside the house, leaving me behind with the dog who was watching my every step. As soon as I walked through the sliding-glass doorway, the dog was close on my heels. Gladys suggested I sit down. Then she disappeared, again leaving me with the dog. As I looked around the large room for somewhere to sit, I couldn't help but notice all her Native artwork. It was then that I decided to sit on a small sofa, watching the dog watch me. Once seated, he walked over and sat down on the floor a couple feet in front of me, staring up as though he had something important to say. He did: I was in his seat. I got up and moved over on the sofa. The dog jumped up beside me, turned around a couple of times, and finally sat down in a position most suitable to keeping an eye on me until Gladys arrived with coffee.

Eventually, Gladys did return. "I can see that you are someone who can be trusted, " she said. I thanked her for the compliment but questioned her reasoning, pointing out she had just met me minutes earlier. Gladys replied: "It's the dog, he likes you." She explained that past experience taught her that he growls at people who can't be trusted. And so began my relationship with this outspoken advocate.

When Gladys calls with information, I always do my best to check it out and get back to her as quickly as possible. I don't want to make that damn dog a liar. When she telephoned on a Sunday night before a morning trip north, I paid attention to her rather odd information. Gladys said she had been at a Native Friendship Centre in Vancouver. While there, a strange man she didn't know kept approaching her as she sat quietly talking and drinking coffee. The man kept trying to tell her he had information about the Highway of Tears. Eventually, after having interrupted her a number of times without ever finishing his story, he told her a very unusual story. He said he knew of a young First Nations girl up north who communicates with one of the missing Tears victims; he knew the victim as Nicole. Due to the girl's age and out of respect for her and her family's privacy, I am going to refer to the little girl as Angel.

I had a general idea that Angel lived on a reservation in the Prince George area, but after two days, 900 kilometres, and a number of stops at various Native reserves along the way, I still hadn't found her. I have this same feeling every time I travel onto a reserve. I am uncomfortable. Maybe I was uncomfortable then because of the "No Trespassing" signs making it clear that outsiders weren't welcome, or maybe because I have a good understanding about why Aboriginal people have such a longstanding mistrust of police, and whites in general. However, although I've often felt somewhat ill at ease on these uninvited visits, I have never received any verbal abuse or experienced any form of intimidation; in fact, almost everyone I've encountered has been helpful and polite. My discomfort, of course, is unimportant, but I was certainly relieved when I eventually confirmed that, although I hadn't found Angel, I had unknowingly found my way onto her grandmother's reserve.

As I waited inside the band office reception area, something strange happened. Despite the fact that no one there knew me or knew why I was there, people began walking by and smiling at me. Others poked their heads out of their work stations to check me out. The band office is usually the location where the reserve's leaders and supporting bureaucracy function. It's often also a social gathering place where community members can get a cup of tea or coffee. Without ever admitting any knowledge of the existence of a little girl named Angel, someone gave me the name of a woman I should speak to and where to find her. This lady turned out to be Angel's grandmother.

A short drive later I found myself where Angel's grandmother worked. When Grandma entered the reception area, before either of us had a chance to speak, she pulled a tissue out of her sweater pocket and began to wipe tears from her eyes. Before introducing myself, I told her that although I may not look all that friendly, no one had ever cried upon meeting me. Grandma didn't laugh. So I introduced myself and told her Gladys's story about Angel and her ability to commune with Nicole Hoar. I immediately questioned the soundness of what I was doing but when I finished, Grandma, who hadn't said a word, put the tissue back in her pocket and apologized. Then she invited me to her private office where she encouraged me to relate my entire story, from start to finish, without her ever confirming she was Angel's grandmother.

After my story she explained that on the previous Sunday, at about the same time Gladys phoned me, she had called her granddaughter. Angel lives on another reserve to the south, and her grandmother always tries to call her on Sundays. She told me this Sunday phone call was different. Angel was excited about something. At first Grandma thought the excitement was about surprise tickets she received from her dad to her first NHL game in Vancouver. Angel couldn't stop talking about all the people, colourful lights, the deafening noise as fans tried to outshout the music, but she never mentioned the actual game. When Grandma asked why, Angel responded: "Why would I watch the game? I already knew who was going to win."

Then Grandma said something that almost knocked me off my chair. In the middle of their conversation about the hockey game, Angel casually asked if the man had come to talk to her yet. Grandma, who had no idea what she was talking about, asked: "What man?" Angel, growing impatient, replied: "You know! The man!" Grandma asked her about the man again so Angel told her the man was going to speak to her about Nicole.

These days it's not hard to turn on the television and find programs dealing with the paranormal, psychics, the spirit world, extrasensory perception or super-intuitiveness, clairvoyance, and communication with the dead. University Professor Dr. Christopher French, of London, England, has extensively studied the paranormal and said most of the skeptics he respects wouldn't say: "We know that paranormal forces don't exist."[10] In one British study, sixty-three percent of those polled said it is possible to know what someone else is thinking or feeling even if they are out of touch by ordinary means; fifty-four percent believe some people can remember past lives; and thirty-seven percent feel it's possible to get messages from the dead.[11] On the other side of the pond, seventy-three percent of all Americans openly admit to having at least one paranormal belief.[12]

Up to that point in my life I was happy to privately embrace a personal belief that I am irregularly intuitive. Intuition is often described by cops as a "gut feeling," but that's as far as I had been prepared to go. I had chosen a practical meat-and-potatoes approach to my life and work, and that was that. However, this started to change when I met Angel and her grandmother. I was compelled to open my mind to other possibilities that in the past I just brushed aside.

I've always believed my investigative success comes from my ability to get people to help me. A big part of my role is to listen without judging and take information from wherever I can, and if some information comes from a paranormal source, so be it. Unfortunately, some of my would-be psychic helpers mistakenly believe my willingness to listen gives them validation. As a result, they are attracted to me like paperclips to a magnet. Over the course of my Tears investigation, I have received information from over sixty psychics from all over the world. Although none of their information to date has helped, some of it has sure been interesting.

As a result of Angel's communications with Nicole, she was able to draw me a spot on a map, indicating an area associated with the case. Although I have never been able to find the *exact* location, her drawing would certainly guide me later in the investigation. But at this stage, I wasn't yet certain where.

———

By the end of 2006 I organized a plan to get more tips. First, I put together a poster showing the names of all Tears victims and the date they went missing or were murdered. I then distributed the poster to all provincial correctional facilities in BC. This, combined with the small notices I placed in local newspapers and the free media coverage I was getting from sources in such places as Prince George, Smithers and Terrace, led to many more leads.

In March of the following year I mailed dozens of letters to people whose homes were located within a large circle surrounding the intersection of Gauthier Road and Highway 16, the area where Nicole had gone missing. I also sent letters to all residents in the immediate vicinity of the property which was once owned by the Switzer brothers' parents. I never received a response from either effort so I decided to focus elsewhere.

I still had Angel's map and referred to it now and then. And then it struck me. Many police investigators who are forced to face the fact that a psychic came up with crucial information on a case will simply explain it away by saying that the psychic "just got lucky." I remained open-minded, and finally realized that the location shown on Angel's hand-drawn map coincided with an area on Norman Lake Road that Leland Switzer described in his taped conversation with police. I located it—a six-kilometre area along that road—and felt compelled to search it.

After examining the site myself, I realized it was too large for one person to thoroughly search. A bigger, multi-person search was required. I knew I could count on a few locals to help, friends I made as a result of my many trips to Prince George, but there still wouldn't be enough people. I contacted Prince George Search and Rescue, who politely told me they were unable to help. I later found out that search-and-rescue efforts must first get the okay from local police. Whether this was an issue I'm not sure.

Out of desperation I asked the two major Prince George newspapers if they would run a story with the date, time and location of my planned search and the need for volunteers to help me conduct it. Before I did that, though, I made an appointment to meet the staff sergeant in charge of the British Columbia Unsolved Homicide Unit and Project E-PANA to let him know I would be conducting a ground search off Highway 16, west of Prince George, for anything related to Nicole Hoar. As usual he politely listened while making notes. Finally, he said he didn't think there was anything the force could or would do to assist. I didn't tell him I had already approached search and rescue; I assumed he already knew that. Nor did I tell him that long before I spoke to anyone about my search intentions, I first talked to Nicole's father.

I couldn't imagine anything in poorer taste than organizing a search for the remains of a family's loved one and not personally consulting with them first. So I telephoned Nicole's parents in Alberta. During our call I explained my theory and reasons for wanting to do a search on Norman Lake Road, but more importantly, I made sure they didn't object to my plan and understood that the search was a very, very long shot. I also knew the search would generate some media attention. At the time, though, I had no idea how much attention it would receive.

Shortly after my search plan appeared in an *Edmonton Sun* article by Gary Castagna, RCMP Staff Sergeant Bruce Hulan telephoned me. He urgently requested a meeting, but this time not in a coffee shop. No, this time in his office. If I hadn't already suspected he had a problem with my search when he called, his demeanour when he met me in his office was a dead giveaway. Although he was attempting to engage in small talk—the kind of small talk cops use to build rapport and loosen the lips of those they are about to interrogate—I could sense he was angry.

Although he didn't say it, I got the impression that he thought Nicole's parents had first learned about my search plans from the newspaper. If that's what he thought, he was wrong. But no matter, the real problem with me going public with my plan and asking for volunteers was that I had no control over how many people, if any, would show up. I soon realized that if I was going to seriously organize a search for Nicole, I would require some additional basic necessities, and that included bathroom facilities. I reached out to Prince George's Port-A-John which volunteered to deliver a number of portable toilets to the search site. Around the same time, the owner of Phoenix Traffic Control Services in Prince George telephoned me saying his firm would volunteer personnel to safely direct traffic off Highway 16 to the site.

People were now calling from as far away as Alberta and

Vancouver asking to help. Staff Sergeant John Ward, on the other hand, told media that although they were aware of the search, they didn't believe there was any reason for it. A little later, the same staff sergeant said that they didn't like what I was doing but would have an officer on-site to contain the scene, if by incredible chance it became a crime scene. Then he gave me credit for being altruistic but typically proceeded to criticize me, suggesting that my actions were very dangerous because I was unfairly raising expectations.[13]

The day before the search, I was invited to a meeting with Staff Sergeant Quinton Smith, the Mountie in charge of the Prince George Major Crime Unit. On second thought, "invited" is far too benign a word. There I sat in a Prince George RCMP detachment interview room surrounded by the staff sergeant and three of his subordinates. I was being grilled about why I was conducting the search. So I mentioned Leland Switzer. The staff sergeant became agitated, telling me Leland Switzer had nothing to do with Nicole Hoar's disappearance. He then grumbled something about how I kept trying to inject myself into the investigation.

As our meeting came to an end, the staff sergeant made it clear that although the RCMP was not officially participating in the search, he, like Staff Sergeant Ward, intended to have one of his members on-site. In addition, he had a list of very specific things that should be done if or when one of the searchers discovered anything of significance. He also made it clear he was holding me personally responsible for the activities of all searchers—in other words, all responsibility was on *me*.

On leaving his office I received a telephone call from a psychic I knew. She wanted to attend the search site, but alone, not with the other searchers. I agreed on the condition that I accompanied her and with the understanding that under no circumstances was she to pick up anything on-site, in compliance with one of the staff sergeant's requirements. We arranged a time to meet but when I arrived early, as I usually do for appointments, her car was parked and she was wandering around the site. When I approached she held out her open hand which held bone fragments. When I reminded her about our prior conversation, she shrugged and gave me the pieces. What a mess. After she showed me where she had *approximately* found the fragments and I marked the location and took a GPS reading, I made the dreaded call to Staff Sergeant Smith. It was only a few hours since he had given me explicit instructions about handling found items and it would certainly appear to him that I was already ignoring these orders. Not surprisingly, he was furious and immediately told me to bring him the bone fragments.

I was soon met by Smith and a coroner at the detachment. The air was thick with fury. The two men examined the fragments, eventually coming to the conclusion they were animal, not human.

I was disappointed and relieved at the same time. Because the fragments were of no significance to the investigation, I didn't feel the need to fully explain how I came into their possession. Staff Sergeant Smith then insisted the three of us go into his office. As he closed the door, his voice intensified and grew louder and louder, and he grew angrier and angrier. He leaned closer and closer toward me and by now his large shaved head had turned completely red and looked on the verge of exploding. I had a sinking feeling he wanted to vault over his desk and hit me. He didn't, choosing instead the more civilized route of threating that if I didn't comply with his instructions from now on, he would see that I lost my PI license.

I left his office and went straight back to Grandma's Inn, reminding myself over and over about why I became involved in the Highway of Tears in the first place. As I sat in my room feeling sorry for myself, the shrill sound of my cellphone interrupted my increasing despair. Dean Price, a Prince George businessman and search-and-rescue (SAR) volunteer, wanted to hear a little about how I was planning the next day's efforts. He asked if I would be interested in meeting with him and veteran SAR volunteer Jeff Smedley to discuss my plans. For those who don't know, SAR training is developed and coordinated by the Emergency Management Division of the Justice Institute of British Columbia (JIBC) and provides an overview of all aspects of ground search and rescue. The training includes in-depth coverage of basic skills such as map and compass, as well as first-aid training, mock searches, overnight snow-cave exercises, rope, swift water, ice rescue, avalanche and tracking.[14]

The two men arrived a few hours later. It was obvious they were feeling me out to determine my motives, deciding whether they would help or not. Jeff ultimately decided while making a few things clear: they would be helping on their own time; their involvement had nothing to do with SAR; and he was used to doing things his way. I got the impression that doing things his way was a deal breaker. I agreed.

I can read a map and use a compass, but if left alone in the middle of the bush I would be lost. But by the end of the meeting I had completed my first introduction to "search and rescue for dummies," and it soon became very apparent that these two guys were about to save me from what could have easily become public humiliation—or worse. Before Jeff and Dean left, I had a rough draft of a "search sign-in sheet" so I could keep track of searchers, something that never occurred to me. I was also told that before the search began, all volunteers would be required to produce photo ID, provide their contact and next of kin information, and provide their signature acknowledging that they were in fact who they said they were. If they didn't comply, they didn't search. I also had a rough draft of an "assignment sheet" that each team leader (who was chosen beforehand) would be given. It included the general search location, the search team's assigned number, a list of team members and whether they carried cellphones, a compass or a GPS unit. This sheet also included columns to record what, if anything, was found, where it was found and who found it. All I had to do was design the two sheets on my computer and print them on my portable printer, a job which lasted long into the night but kept my thoughts focused on the following day—and off Sergeant Smith.

At six the next morning I arrived at the search site, forty-two kilometres west of Prince George, south of Highway 16. The Port-A-Johns had already been delivered and set up, as promised. Jeff and Dean were already there preparing the search grid for my anticipated volunteers, something I had never thought of either. After dividing the map into search areas labelled A, B, C, D, etc., the pair disappeared into the bush with GPS units to mark the grids with orange vinyl flagging. This would help ensure that the searchers stayed within their assigned areas.

The volunteers began arriving at 8:00 a.m., as did a member of Staff Sergeant Smith's investigation team. His job was to ensure that any evidence was properly handled. The search was also attended by a coroner and an anthropologist from the University of Northern BC, an off-duty RCMP member, several media personnel from as far away as Calgary, First Nations people from a nearby reserve, a number of psychics, a man who was well known for his water-witching (dowsing) abilities, and another who was known to be quite proficient at finding items using a pendulum. In total, over 100 people came to volunteer their time. The searchers were divided into groups of approximately ten, and each group assigned a search area that they covered at arm's length, walking from one end of the grid to the other, then from one predesignated grid to another.

One searcher said the Tears situation left people feeling helpless and that the search gave him a chance to take positive action; a woman said she was passing through the area with her husband on an RV trip when they heard about the search and decided to stop and volunteer; another said she was there because if it were her daughter, she would want people to help out too; and during a break another approached me, wiping away tears and saying she wanted to thank me on behalf of all families of women who were missing and for making it possible for her to do something to help.[16]

A reporter later said that if I was feeling the pressure to prove my hunch, I wasn't showing it.[17] I didn't feel pressure, but by now I was obsessed with the Highway of Tears and would have been haunted till my death if I hadn't conducted the search out of any potential embarrassment that it might have caused me. The truth is, I was so stressed out worrying about the RCMP and what might go wrong on the search, that when Nicole's father introduced himself I didn't immediately realize who he was.

Jack Hoar and I had earlier discussed the possibility of he and his family attending the search. I made it clear that finding anything of value was a long shot; nonetheless, Jack and his wife and daughter had come a long way to be there with what must have been an enormous amount of anxiety. And there I was, so stressed out I didn't even recognize him. What an idiot.

By the end of the search over 110 bone fragments had been found. They were subsequently inspected; none were human. One searcher concluded she was glad she had participated, but sad because nothing was found.[18] The RCMP member on-site politely said they could now rule out the area as a possible crime scene.[19] I could hear RCMP laughter all the way from Vancouver.

After the search I mailed a letter to every one of the 100-plus individuals who had helped, thanking them for their assistance and asking them to copy my letter and pass it on in the event I missed anyone.

———

By mid-December 2008 I had established a twenty-four-hour, toll-free tip line for the Highway of Tears cases. It would no longer be necessary for tipsters to call long distance just to phone me.

To promote the new number, I created an email flyer asking for information on some persons of interest. I sent the flyer to 120 Aboriginal organizations from Prince Rupert across the north to 100 Mile House, my largest mass communication project to date.

In September of that year I decided to follow up on a tip received in an anonymous letter. It cited a local rumour that Nicole had been seen on the Tachet Reserve just after she disappeared and the vehicle she had been travelling in was abandoned at the Tachet ball field. The semi-isolated community of Tachet is approximately an hour's drive northwest of Burns Lake, near Topley Landing. Tachet Reserve is found at the mouth of the Fulton River on Babine Lake, the second largest body of freshwater in British Columbia. The Nedut'en people live in one of the five communities of the Lake Babine Nation, the third largest First Nations band in the province. When I arrived in Tachet, after unsuccessfully attempting to locate the ball field, I went to the community-owned Tachet Trapper's Gas Store. Although I had a problem finding the ball field I would have had to be blind not to locate Trapper's on Main Street. There was a huge gas storage tank with metal steps up one side. The building itself was a log structure, probably once a trapper's cabin, painted brown with a green roof and trim. Its entrance was hidden behind the giant gas tank. Just inside the door and off to the right were the store's counter and cash register.

I said hello to the lady behind the counter and continued farther into the one-room store. The counter space and walls were covered with groceries, confectionary, Native handmade crafts and everything else you'd expect in a northern convenience store. Maybe I was paranoid, but it seemed the only thing out of place was me as I was sure I could feel the clerk watching my every move. Yet it was a friendly place and with her help, I eventually found the Tachet ball field by following vehicle tracks in the grass over a small bush-covered hill. Except for the field's mesh backstop, you would never have known the place was once a ball diamond.

The overgrown field was home to a dozen or more abandoned vehicles, left there for locals to salvage. Eventually, I located the suspect vehicle in the middle of a number of other wrecks. After I recorded the vehicle identification number (VIN) and took pictures, I headed west to Smithers.

When I eventually got back home to Vancouver I sent flyers containing Nicole's picture to every address in that small community, asking people to call, write or email if they had ever seen her in the area. I also forwarded the tip I received, the VIN of the vehicle, and the pictures I had taken to the RCMP in Prince George. The flyer was a dud, and I never heard back from E-PANA investigators about the vehicle.

To someone accustomed to coming and going behind the scenes, as though I wasn't ever there in the first place, I now no longer enjoyed the benefits of living in the shadows. I had become recognized, "that guy," the "crazy white man" investigating the Tears cases. For my efforts, I had gained a First Nations grandmother's trust, and met a psychic teenager whose visions for the first time in my life unwittingly forced me to seriously consider the meanings of spirituality. I had survived a search I was initially wholly unprepared for, but thanks to the efforts of two strangers who, without me having to ask, volunteered their expertise and saved the day. I suffered the wrath of the RCMP and came to a big dead end in an overgrown ball field 1,300 kilometres from my home. I had been put through the wringer, yet despite all the wacky twists and turns, false starts and disappointment, I felt more determined to solve these cases than ever before.

10. WHO IS RAMONA WILSON?

"I never once felt any false hope that Ray would find these people ... he gave me hope to start healing and thinking how things can be done differently so these tragedies do not need to happen again. "—Brenda Wilson

First Nations teenager Ramona Wilson was born, raised and went to school in Smithers. She was sixteen when she disappeared on June 1, 1994 while hitchhiking to nearby Moricetown to visit her boyfriend. Her body was found nearly a year later in a bushy area to the west of Smithers Airport. Ramona's mother, Matilda, once dared to ask something that many families of other murdered and missing Aboriginal women across Western Canada have been thinking all these years: How would my child's investigation have been handled had she been blue-eyed and blonde?

Ramona's friend once described her as a young woman with hopes and dreams for the future, someone with more drive than anyone else her age. She said Ramona had taught her that things happen for a reason and the Creator has a purpose for everyone and everything. Unfortunately, Ramona's friend continues to struggle about the purposelessness of Ramona's murder.

My investigation revealed Ramona was last seen when she stopped at a party on her way to Moricetown. The gathering was in one of the old ramshackle duplexes along the highway, east of Smithers Airport and across the street from Kathlyn Lake; this information was confirmed to me by an anonymous RCMP investigator. The buildings were well known to locals, including police, but have long since been demolished following a fire, leaving a large empty field overlooking the lake.

In March of 2008 I interviewed a First Nations man who told me he had been a witness to Ramona's death, described what had happened, and gave me the name of a suspect and witnesses. He also said he was not the first to try to tell someone about her death. A few years earlier, a woman who had also said she had been a witness to the crime had gone to Smithers RCMP to tell them what she had seen. She was arbitrarily dismissed as crazy and told she didn't know what she was talking about. The man also said this witness has since died, with no attention ever given to her information.

The male witness took me to the alleged crime scene and to the location of the now-wrecked suspected vehicle thought to have been used in the crime. He agreed to relate his story to the RCMP, so I drove to the Smithers detachment. We were greeted by a couple of polite young police officers. After I explained who I was and why I was there, one of the officers asked: "Who is Ramona Wilson?"

Smithers, with a population of about 4,500 is Ramona Wilson's hometown. She grew up there. She went to school there, it was the town she had disappeared from and where her body had been found a year later, and yet I had to explain to the police who Ramona

Wilson was. This was inexplicable.

Just when I thought I couldn't be more surprised, one of the young cops told me the Highway of Tears had nothing to do with them, that it was Vancouver's case. I asked if there was a plainclothes member (detective) I could talk to. Before either of them could answer, we were interrupted by a civilian employee who came around the corner and asked if I had an appointment. When I told her I didn't, she said I would have to make one and come back later. I ignored her, quietly explaining to the young cops that the man who was standing behind me was a potential witness to a cold-case crime. He wanted to tell them his story now and if denied that opportunity and forced to make an appointment, he might change his mind. Someone needed to talk to him now.

There I was, standing in a police office with a potentially credible witness and maybe the first and only big break in Ramona Wilson's case, waiting for the cops' decision on whether to interview him. I was near speechless, something that doesn't happen too often. I was also on the verge of exploding. Then the cops agreed to interview him while the civilian employee disappeared around a corner.

I left the man at the police office and returned to my motel. I couldn't help but remember that it had taken me over half a year once I began my Tears investigation before I could get the RCMP to talk to me. Countless people had been telling me they had repeatedly tried to give information to the police, only to be ignored or told to call long distance somewhere else, never to hear back from them again. Having left the potential witness in the hands of the Smithers detachment, I was worried there was about to be a screw up, so I decided to call Staff Sergeant Bruce Hulan, the head of E-PANA, to let him know what had just happened. The call did nothing to alleviate my worry. The staff sergeant came across as surprised, if not shocked, so I followed up with an email explaining where the suspect vehicle that the potential witness had showed me was abandoned. I never received a reply to the email.

I don't know why Hulan sounded surprised. Perhaps it was because he didn't expect me to make that kind of progress. Or perhaps it was because in 2005, now-RCMP Commissioner Bob Paulson had organized a group of police specialists to review a few Tears cases. Their conclusion? That Ramona Wilson, Roxanne Thiara, and Leah Germaine appeared to have been murdered by the same individual.[2] I realized for the first time that it was possible E-PANA's theory was based on that 2005 conclusion. I had no idea what, if any, influence Bob Paulson had on their investigation. I do know he was once described as a "strong-willed person when it came to his idea about conducting major investigations."[3] I also believe my discovery had the potential to put the RCMP's Tears investigative theory into question. Perhaps, similar to their Air

India investigation, the RCMP "prematurely dismissed information on the basis of preliminary assessments of credibility."[4]

The RCMP called me to pick the man up. As I drove him home, I was concerned that the suspect in Ramona's case, someone from the man's community, would find out about his trip to the police thereby jeopardizing his safety. He told me an RCMP officer had asked him: "Do you own a rifle?" But before he could reply, the Mounties casually suggested since everyone on "The Rez" owns one, he must. When he admitted he did own a rifle, the cops told him he had a right to defend himself. I was worried about this witness's safety and the police's cavalier attitude. I suggested dropping him off a few blocks from his residence, but he calmly—and proudly—told me he felt he had done the right thing and wasn't worried, so I reluctantly dropped him off in his driveway.

When I returned home I did some quick research on the potential suspect. I discovered that dating back as far as 2001, he had a number of encounters with the law, including a proceeding to terminate an order to comply with the *Sex Offender Information Registration Act*.[5] A person's past transgressions don't necessarily make them guilty of other crimes, but in my opinion, these should be considered "red flags" to investigators.

Ramona Wilson's murder was still unsolved a year later. It was about this time I received a phone call from a woman who thought I should know what a hitchhiker once told her on Highway 16 west of Smithers. He said he had a name of a suspect in Ramona's murder, as well as the names of other witnesses to her death, and had passed this on to the RCMP, as well as information about himself. He said he was so upset about the lack of RCMP action on the matter that every time he is picked up hitchhiking along the highway he retells his entire story, naming the possible suspects and witnesses to whoever will listen. When I passed this information on to Staff Sergeant Hulan, he told me they were already aware of this person's behaviour and would have to talk with him. About time, I thought to myself.

———

A few days after Frank Peebles of *The Prince George Citizen* quoted me as saying, "I said in January I was optimistic about the year ahead, well I'm even more so now," the RCMP released a statement on its website on behalf of E-PANA. The headline read "E-PANA Investigators Clarify Misinformation;" the subtitle read, "E-PANA Investigators clarify misinformation in media coverage involving Private Investigator Ray Michalko." One of the things the RCMP said they wanted to set straight was their belief that there were recent reports "misrepresenting the status" of one of their files. But they did not clarify which file they were referring to. They also pointed out that they were "in the best position to determine the speed, flow and direction of the investigations." They described the E-PANA investigation as one of the "larger ongoing projects in BC," an investigation involving the original jurisdictions that worked the cases.

A dozen news stories followed, including the RCMP's assertion that if investigative information became public, it "might give the accused a head start." As far as giving an accused a "head start,"[6] with respect to Ramona Wilson's case, her killer had already been given a fourteen-year head start, which makes you wonder.

Several months later I learned from the man that I brought in for the interview that no one else, including E-PANA investigators, had spoken to or re-interviewed him. E-PANA investigators did not request that he submit to a polygraph test to help determine credibility; they did not accompany him to the possible crime scene; no one asked him to show them where the potential suspect's truck, possibly used at the time of the crime, was located; and to the best of his knowledge, investigators had not attempted to interview the potential suspect.

I decided to follow up with the potential witness and begin my own investigation. I didn't want to do that if it would hinder or interfere with any investigation the RCMP might be doing behind the scenes so I sent a registered letter to Staff Sergeant Hulan. I sent it registered because I wanted to have something on record showing he received it. In the letter I explained that I would be working in the

Smithers-Moricetown area sometime during the last week of April or the first week of May 2008. During that time, unless the RCMP had specific objections, I planned to interview the suspect who had been named by the potential witness I had previously brought forward. I also requested that if Hulan had any objections that he notify me in writing, in a timely enough manner for me to review his objections and make arrangements to discuss them with him prior to my trip north.

Hulan responded approximately one week later: "On behalf of the RCMP I wanted to express our sincere gratitude for identifying a person who states he has information related to the death of Ramona Wilson." The letter continued: "On the basis of your former police experience as well as your current professional capacity as a private investigator, I have no doubt you are aware the investigation of a homicide is a complex matter. The investigation is ongoing, the focus of homicide investigations constantly changes and an independent investigator, unaware of all the facts, may in spite of best intentions adversely impact the investigation, or profoundly jeopardize the safety of potential witnesses." The letter concluded by asking that I not contact the potential witness I had located or "take any action that in any way might characterize an investigation into the death of Ramona Wilson."

I replied in writing, agreeing not to interview the potential suspect. I also explained that my Tears investigation was public knowledge and as such, I was receiving calls from the public on a weekly basis. I informed him that I was consequently unable to comply with his request not to take action in regard to Ramona's death or any of the other Highway 16 cases.

A few days later I received a written reply from Staff Sergeant Hulan, reiterating that the RCMP was grateful that I was passing information along, something they hoped would continue. That was the carrot, followed by the hammer: "Indeed, your reluctance to comply with my request that you do not take any action that might in any way be characterized as an investigation into the death of Ramona Wilson continues to cause me concern, and to that end I must advise you that your conduct with respect to this investigation could adversely affect and obstruct the investigation to the extent that it could defeat the course of justice. I would ask that you carefully reconsider my concern, and in doing so review Section 139 of the *Criminal Code of Canada*." This section of the Criminal Code deals with a couple of situations, including one where someone wilfully attempts to obstruct, pervert or defeat the course of justice. The penalty, imprisonment for a term not exceeding ten years.[7]

I am of the opinion that when you feel RCMP tactics toward you are unfair, it's to your advantage to go public. In early May I spoke with Ryan Jensen, a reporter for the Smithers *Interior News* who worked up the story. "The RCMP could decide to take this course of action at any time in the future," I told him, "making it impossible for me to continue, except under the threat of the possibility of being charged with a *Criminal Code* offence." Jensen's article suggested the circumstances surrounding the RCMP's threat to charge me with a *Criminal Code* offence "smack of hypocrisy." He also noted the RCMP had said they were committed to finding the person or persons responsible for the killings, and it was they who wanted to be the ones to bring them to justice.[8] That month the same newspaper started a poll on its website: "Should PI Ray Michalko Halt His Investigation into the Highway of Tears?" Eighty-nine percent voted "No."

I decided to ask Norman Groot of Investigation Counsel in Toronto for advice. Groot is the author of *Canadian Law and Private Investigations* and I consider him to be the foremost expert on the subject. In May 2008, Groot wrote a letter advising the RCMP he had reviewed Hulan's letter with senior counsel and was "concerned with the authority by which he made his comments." He requested that the RCMP pass along Hulan's threatening letter to Crown Counsel or the RCMP's own counsel, and then advise him "specifically, what conduct or proposed conduct" of mine Hulan was referring to as "criminal." Mr. Groot concluded: "There is no property in witnesses." He added: "To many in your province, it has appeared the RCMP investigation has lacked some intensity."

Staff Sergeant Hulan replied later that month with no reference to ever having consulted with Crown Counsel. Instead, he stuck to his original opinion that any investigation into Ramona Wilson's case by me "could potentially constitute an offence under Section 139 of the *Criminal Code of Canada*."

As a result of this position and the lack of success solving any of the Tears cases, the RCMP was taking a lot of heat in the media. Consequently, I was gaining more trust and respect among First Nations people along Highway 16.

Later that year the RCMP changed their approach. Superintendent Russ Nash, the officer in charge of "E" Division Major Crime Section, wrote an open letter to the editor of the *Interior News* in Smithers: "I would like to take this opportunity to correct a misconception in news briefs and editorials I have read recently about the way in which Private Investigator Mr. Ray Michalko has been treated by the Royal Canadian Mounted Police, in connection with E-PANA Highway 16 investigative review." The letter explained that a large team of dedicated investigators was reviewing several files involving missing and murdered women in Northern and Central BC. "It is also important to recognize that the RCMP is appreciative of the information that Mr. Michalko has provided to our investigators. We are very thankful for information provided by any citizen in relation to an ongoing investigation or criminal activity and do our best to bring the issues raised to a successful conclusion."

Superintendent Nash wrote that it was "truly unfortunate this situation has become a topic of recent news articles and broadcasts." He also noted: "There are now those with the false impression the RCMP may harbour ill feelings against Mr. Michalko for his personal involvement in attempting to gather witnesses or evidence that may be of assistance to our investigation. The truth is that I applaud Mr. Michalko's commitment and resolve and am certain the families of those victims, both missing and murdered, are equally appreciative. It must be stressed, however, that his role as a private citizen is much different than the role of a police officer."

Superintendent Nash concluded by assuring the public: "The RCMP are absolutely committed to this investigation and continue to expend extraordinary human and financial resources towards the resolution of these important investigations." He urged me to "continue to provide information to our investigators…" However, he also stated that the RCMP were asking "that his good intentions as a private citizen not impede the progress of our investigation."[9]

I was on vacation in Washington State when I received a call from Prince George newspaper reporter Frank Peebles. When Frank asked me what I thought about the support I was getting from some of the Tears families and the upcoming news conference, I asked: "What news conference?" To my surprise, family members of some of the victims had publicly come to my defence. Ramona Wilson's mother Matilda had called her local newspaper. "[Michalko] takes the time to keep close contact with us," she told the paper. "That's very important for us, because we know he's out there trying to solve this. We have hope now that he's working on this." The RCMP team, she said, "updates the families every six months. The content of their message is expected, but the delivery simply lacks Michalko's touch." She added: "It would be so sad if they [RCMP] had to bump him out of what he's doing ... I'm pretty sure the RCMP are working very hard on the case, but what I'm saying right now is: To eliminate Ray Michalko out of the investigation would just make things really complicated again. The people involved— especially the victims' parents—would be devastated. If I learned that he was going, I wouldn't be able to go on."[11]

—

On November 24, 2008, I initiated a Freedom of Information Request to the RCMP. I wanted to know the total cost of the Highway of Tears investigation from inception to date. I also requested they tell me the size of the operating budget and total cost to date for the RCMP "E" Division E-PANA investigation. After a number of delays the police phoned saying they estimated it would take them approximately 200 hours to determine the total cost to date,

195 hours of which I would have to pay for at a rate of $10 per hour. My second request for the total cost of the RCMP "E" Division E-PANA investigation would only take five hours, and there would be no charge for this information.

I decided to forgo spending the $1,950 and instead opted for the free information. It was a good choice. Early the following year a Lower Mainland newspaper reported that the E-PANA investigative team's operating budget had been boosted from $2.1 million to $3.6 million.[12] After the RCMP made this information public, I received a letter from them regarding my Freedom of Information request. It spelled out the amount as per their news release.

Ironically, in October 2012 I received an email from an RCMP E-PANA investigator. Because I believe this individual is still an active member of the RCMP I am keeping his name confidential. The purpose of the email was to let me know that Ramona Wilson's team of investigators was working toward their final investigational stages, whatever that meant. In the midst of that process, they were concerned about whether they had missed anything, in particular a potential witness I may have discovered. The email explained that the police had interviewed several witnesses and persons of interest who had told them I had interviewed them as well. As a result, investigators were "curiously wondering" if the information these individuals relayed to me was consistent with what they received. "In an effort to feel confident we have spoken to everyone who has any knowledge of the various files and in the event we have missed anyone," the E-PANA investigator wrote, "it would be beneficial to all concerned if we were aware of the existence of any potential evidence, witnesses, the individual identities and the information which they may possess." I was asked if I would be willing to meet with the letter-writer and several key members of the team to discuss their concerns and to solicit my assistance in solving this and perhaps other E-PANA files.

The proposed meeting made perfect sense from an investigator's point of view, but I doubted the RCMP's Executive Branch would see it that way. I couldn't help but think about John Ward, my old North Vancouver RCMP detachment friend who made the mistake of publicly admitting he knew me, something that from a police management point of view gave me credibility. The RCMP brass would certainly see it like this as well. So it didn't make much difference that a collaboration of sorts made sense. It was simply not the RCMP's way of doing things. I agreed to the meeting, but it never took place.

By the end of December I had exchanged a couple more emails with the E-PANA investigator. He wrote that he would touch base with me in the New Year. He never did. My efforts to contact him by email, telephone, and a personal visit to his office were unsuccessful. For some reason, he decided touching base was no longer a good idea.

11. DON'T CALL THAT PI

"In principle the end issue of this tragedy is more justice, for if any perpetrator escapes justice it is that much easier for him to do it again, and again, and again ..."
— Reverend Lloyd Thomas of the Bethel First Baptist Church, Prince Rupert, BC, taken from his summary of events regarding Tamara Chipman's disappearance

Twenty-two-year-old Tamara Chipman was an Aboriginal single mother who was last seen hitchhiking on Highway 16, east of Prince Rupert near an industrial park. It was around 4:30 p.m. on Wednesday, September 21, 2005. Tamara's father Tom described his daughter as outgoing and confident, the type of person who "wasn't one to take too much crap from people."[1] Tom said his tall, slim daughter was hard to miss. And her family also believed it was out of character for her to hitchhike, especially along the highway. Yet she was known to police due to a couple minor run-ins with them, so the family had hoped she might have just been "lying low from the law." Terrace RCMP Staff Sergeant Eric Stubbs characterized Tamara as an individual who led a "high-risk lifestyle." He also said that ten police officers were treating her case as a missing person investigation, without ruling out foul play. Going forward, investigators would rely on tips from the public and focus their attention along what they described as "the highway and its infamous past."[2] Tamara's father also organized search parties that combed the highway between Prince Rupert and Terrace, but to no avail.

Retired South African pastor Lloyd Thomas, who was temporarily living and working in Prince Rupert as pastor of the Bethel First Baptist Church, said Tamara had been "slandered with the same connotations that befell other previous Tears victims." Often, a Tears victim was "written off by many as just another Native girl who went to Vancouver to make good money working the streets." But those close to Tamara knew she would never abandon her son. In an email to me, Lloyd Thomas wrote that by the end of 2005 rumours surrounding her death began to circulate. Prince George RCMP, 700 kilometres to the east, took over the investigation. But nothing substantial surfaced.

Prior to personally meeting Reverend Thomas I received a telephone call telling me an almost unbelievable story about a potential witness to Tamara's murder. Keeping in mind that up to this point she was a missing person not a murder victim, I listened intently to what the caller had to say. Our conversation involved a request for my assistance dealing with this female potential witness. I decided that due to the nature of the information and its potential to help solve the case, the RCMP should be involved as quickly as possible. When I first suggested this the caller was reluctant to involve the police because, as he put it, they wouldn't do *F — All*. I asked if he knew any local cops he could talk to without being brushed off. He said he knew one and told me he would give him a call, even though he thought it was a waste of time. I made a suggestion: if he got the impression the police were reluctant to get involved, he should tell them he would call that PI from Vancouver. I suspected that was the last thing the RCMP wanted to hear. As I understand it, he followed my suggestion and was told by police that they would look into it, and whatever he did, he was not to call me.

In 2007, Reverend Thomas said he obtained what he described as "explicit, confidential information regarding Tamara's disappearance." The information came from a woman he described as a "very uncooperative long-term drug user suffering from liver damage and hepatitis C." She had "been taken to hospital to be treated for extreme hysteria as a result of flashbacks caused by participating in Tamara's murder." The RCMP had been contacted but the young woman wouldn't talk. It was also rumoured that a motorcycle gang had put "a hit out on her," so she was placed in protective custody.

The doctor in charge of the woman's case suggested to police that the local pastor—in this case Lloyd Thomas—attempt to act as an agent or intermediary between the law and patient. Thomas was contacted the next day. A room was arranged in the medical clinic for the meeting and the woman escorted there from a local hotel by three RCMP members who had been guarding her. The next day at 9:00 a.m. a second meeting took place in a local motel. The pastor, armed with photographs of Tamara, a digital tape recorder, bottled water and donuts, all compliments of the RCMP, conducted the interview. During the three-hour tape-recorded session, the possible witness eventually named the primary suspect. The woman also shared graphic details of Tamara's death. By noon, after listening to the brutal details, Thomas had to get out of the motel room. In the elevator, he and the woman were joined by three plainclothes Mounties who then followed them as they drove to the locations along Highway 16 that had been described during the interview.

The woman said she was driving the suspect's late-model K-car on the night Tamara was murdered. Although the suspect owned it, the vehicle was not registered in his name and he didn't have a driver's license. There was one other male in the vehicle. They picked up Tamara outside of town near the industrial area. Tamara had wanted a ride home to Terrace and offered to pay anyone who would take her. Since no one was willing, she resorted to hitchhiking the 140 kilometres. There was no explanation as to how the woman and others in the vehicle located Tamara or if they had been sent by someone to pick her up.

The woman then said Tamara got in the backseat. She sat behind the man in the front passenger seat and beside a second male who was in the seat behind the driver. As soon as they were out of town, the man in the front passenger seat signaled to his partner in the back and together they allegedly murdered Tamara.

The male in the front passenger seat told the driver to turn left toward Kloya Bay so they could dump Tamara's body. There were too many people at that location so they continued east along Highway 16, turning off near Tweedledee-Tweedledum Lakes. The men were in a hurry to return to Prince Rupert to help a friend move from his home before sheriffs seized his possessions. They therefore decided to temporarily hide Tamara's corpse. The man in the backseat was wearing an ankle brace and using crutches to walk, leaving him unable to help. So the woman helped drag Tamara's body into the trees, where she was covered with some dead branches.

The woman then said that when the trio returned to their friend's home, they washed Tamara's blood from their clothing; however, the primary suspect's leather jacket was so saturated it had to be thrown away. The woman said one of the men stole yellow blankets and put them in the trunk of the car, to be used when they returned to better hide the body. After helping their friend move, the trio stayed the night in Prince Rupert, returning to the body the following day.

Thomas said he pushed the female witness for answers, but she became agitated and insisted they return to town. She refused to remain in protective custody, so the pastor dropped her off at a local transition house. They agreed Thomas would pick her up at 9:00 a.m. the following day to continue the search for Tamara's burial site.

The next day the witness was gone. Thomas then said he met with the RCMP. They advised him they were going to have his taped conversation with the witness transcribed; then, in the next few weeks, a warrant would be issued for her arrest.[3]

Thomas contacted the woman's boyfriend, who had told her not to cooperate with the RCMP because they were looking for a scapegoat in Tamara's death. A few days later, the RCMP told Thomas there was a court order preventing the woman's boyfriend from contacting her. They also asked the pastor that if he saw the pair together, would he swear an affidavit to that effect so that the man could be immediately arrested. Less than two weeks later, Thomas found the woman and her boyfriend but was unable to get them to cooperate, so he provided the requested affidavit to police. To the pastor's knowledge, his affidavit was never acted upon. In the meanwhile, the woman had consulted a lawyer who advised her not to say anything more.

Thomas said that on July 11, 2007, a Prince Rupert Mountie told him the RCMP was no longer pursuing inquiries regarding that possible witness, but did not explain why. The pastor then decided that Tamara's family had a right to know what was going on. He approached the Mountie offering to notify Tamara's parents himself. He said he was told not to as it would cause a media circus. Frustrated by the police's unwillingness to do what he thought was the right thing, Thomas eventually located Tamara's father over a month later and gave him the bad news.

On September 27, 2007, the RCMP issued a second-anniversary update regarding Tamara's investigation. They stated their investigators had made significant progress in eliminating a number of tips and were concentrating on some compelling leads. In addition, they said that five days earlier a wooded area east of Prince Rupert had been examined by a trained search-and-rescue team assisted by police. However, no meaningful evidence was uncovered. To date, Tamara's body has never been found.

———

Pastor Thomas said he met with the RCMP in their office four months after having notified Tamara's father and was "reprimanded by a visibly angry RCMP member for what was described as a breach of confidentiality and impeding their investigation." He replied simply that as next of kin, the father had a right to know. Thomas also told me the female who said she was witness to Tamara's murder died in 2010 of causes that "arose from an unnatural lifestyle."

In June 2007 I received a call from a woman living in Vancouver. Her son had been at a party in Courtenay, on Vancouver Island, where he met a woman who told him she had one of Tamara's skirts. She wanted to know if he would like to have it, as he was Tamara's cousin. I decided rather than getting personally involved in what could be significant evidence, I would call the head of E-PANA to pass the information along. Staff Sergeant Hulan told me he would contact the woman who had the skirt. I telephoned her saying the RCMP would contact her, and asked to let me know when they did.

Approximately three weeks later I was driving from an investigation in the Southern Interior. As my mind wandered, a little voice in my head told me the police had not yet contacted the woman. When I returned to Vancouver I called her. That little voice was right: she told me she had not been contacted but was going out of town for the next three weeks, so they wouldn't be able to reach her until then. To save face—for both myself and the RCMP—I made arrangements to pick up the skirt, which I did. I then emailed the staff sergeant with the details. He replied that his team tried contacting the woman, leaving several phone messages that were never returned. The following day a member of the Fraser Valley Unsolved Homicide Unit called me; he wanted to pick up the skirt. By then I had more info on the skirt. The previous night, I talked to Tamara's cousin by phone who told me how the skirt surfaced. Tamara used to live in a basement suite in Terrace. Sometime after she went missing, Tamara's landlord, while getting rid of her things, gave the skirt to the woman at the party, who then gave it to Tamara's cousin. Since the skirt-as-evidence possibility was now a wild-goose chase, the RCMP Unsolved Homicide Unit member and I agreed that I would return it to Tamara's parents.

Part of my role in the Tears investigation is to track down leads and in this case possible evidence. This process doesn't always locate the smoking gun and much of what turns up may be insignificant, but as long as someone like myself, with an open mind, keeps searching and uncovering stories, chasing down leads and looking for evidence, something might just click. The police might not always be vigilant and even though this possible evidence didn't turn out, it shows the need to keep them on their toes, to try and ensure that they follow up on the information I provide.

In the end I finally gave the skirt to Tamara's aunt, Gladys Radek, who had dedicated the following "to my precious niece, Tamara Chipman."

sweet memories

It has been almost a year since you've gone,

The Highway of Tears always on my mind,

Sometimes I wake in the middle of the night,

And see you sitting at the foot of my bed,

You look at me with love in your eyes and say

Can we talk auntie? Or are you too tired?

I give you the answer that you know is true.

Yes, we can talk, never too tired for you.

One night I woke up and felt you in my arms,

You were snuggled so close to me

Passionately sucking your thumb.

I wrapped my arms around you

Told you things will be okay,

You said, I love you auntie,

I said I love you too,

Your big beautiful smile,

How it would brighten up a room,

Your spirit brought love and joy

Happiness in the heart,

Miss you so much baby girl,

Love you with all my heart,

You will always be in my sweet memories.

Lots of Love, Auntie Gladys

Gladys Radek
Wet su wit'en Nation

12. POPEYE'S

"The difference between fiction and reality? Fiction has to make sense."
— Tom Clancy, attributed to an interview on *Larry King Live*

Alberta Williams disappeared from a crowded sidewalk outside the Prince Rupert Hotel in the early morning hours just after it closed. One month later her body was found by hikers about forty kilometres east of Prince Rupert on Highway 16 near the Tyee Overpass. Alberta was twenty-four-years old. At that time, the RCMP said there was no reason to suspect foul play.[1]

In the summer of 1989, Alberta and her sister Claudia moved from Vancouver to work summer jobs at a local fish plant in Prince Rupert. The move made sense because their family lived in town which meant a free place to stay. Work was drawing to a close by the end of August, so Alberta joined her two sisters, a cousin and some friends at Popeye's Pub, in the Prince Rupert Hotel, for a farewell drink. The six-storey, eighty-eight-room Rupert was a popular spot built after the original hotel burned to the ground in 1976.

I first spoke with Claudia Williams in January 2009. She telephoned to ask if I could help her get in touch with anyone in the RCMP so she could attend an upcoming E-PANA meeting. Although it would be the fifth to take place between the police and families since the March 2006 Prince George symposium, no one from Claudia's family had ever been invited.

I gave her the phone number of E-PANA boss Bruce Hulan. Claudia told me she called and left a message for the senior Mountie, eventually receiving a call back from someone in the RCMP who told her they were working on her sister's case. Claudia disagreed, saying she didn't believe they were working on the case as they hadn't even kept in touch with her family. The RCMP then told her to come to their office in Surrey for a video interview to give them all of her information, but she told them she lived in Vancouver and didn't have a car to make the forty-kilometre trip. There was no suggestion of doing an interview at Claudia's home. But she was told they would keep in touch. That was the last time the RCMP talked to Claudia about her sister's murder. Claudia also said that she had previously been contacted by a potential witness claiming to have information about Alberta and the people who may have been responsible for her murder. However, this person was too afraid to go to police. She relayed this information to the cops but told me she had no idea if they ever spoke to her or not.

I decided to meet Claudia after several telephone calls asking for my help. That was April 2010. I felt bad for her. Her family was never invited to any of the E-PANA meetings. More important from an investigative point of view, I thought she had some seriously valuable information that might help move Alberta's case along to an arrest and charges. So I decided to help. Claudia and I now have a written contractual agreement for me to investigate the 1989 homicide of her sister, in consideration of her payment of $1. My company agreed to cover all investigative costs. She signed the contract.

Claudia told me that around 10:00 p.m. the night in question, she and Alberta went to Popeye's for a bit, then to the Cabaret, located in the basement, because she thought there would be a number of people there they knew. Once in the Cabaret, Alberta sat at a big table which was made up of a number of smaller tables pulled together. There were several people sitting there, all of whom she was still easily able to name. Claudia said she didn't sit with the group like her sister but instead wandered around the Cabaret, returning to the table from time to time. She described one of the people at the table as a "red flag," someone who looked like a "real temperamental guy."

Everyone stayed in the Cabaret until Popeye's upstairs closed. Then they went outside to the front of the hotel where quite a few people had already gathered. As the group mingled on the sidewalk, Alberta shouted to Claudia that she was going to a house party at the home of one of the men who had been at the table. Before Claudia could respond, she was momentarily distracted by her ex-boyfriend. When she looked back, Alberta was gone. She went around the corner to see if she was there. Nothing. So she went back to the lobby to check the washroom. Again, not a sign. Claudia then went back outside and waited on the corner for fifteen minutes, but her sister never returned. She then realized that not only had Alberta vanished, but the entire group from the Cabaret had gone as well. Claudia assumed they had all headed to the party, so she instead went back to her brother's house where she had been staying. Three days later Alberta had still not returned. Their father called the police; however, Claudia was never interviewed, then or now.

A few weeks later, Alberta's father invited the man he believed may have been responsible for his daughter's death to his home to talk. Once there the unsuspecting individual was confronted by the father while some community elders sat in the background observing. The father said it hurt him to see the brothers and sisters looking around for Alberta and wanted to know what happened to his daughter. The person appeared nervous, his leg shaking as he denied any knowledge of Alberta's disappearance. This man would become my primary suspect in Alberta's murder.

Claudia also told me that two brothers had been staying at the Prince Rupert home where the party had supposedly taken place. The home was probably the last place Alberta had been seen. She gave me their names along with the name of a third individual who may have specific information about Alberta's death. That said, I managed to locate a Vancouver telephone number for one of the brothers; he was a teenager at the time of the murder. The man said he and his brother had been working at the fish plant in the summer of 1989 and were living in the Prince Rupert home where the party had been held the night Alberta disappeared. He said when he awakened from sleep around 2:00 a.m. to go to the bathroom, he saw Alberta and a number of other individuals, some known to him, sitting around a table drinking. Years later, his brother, who at the time had slept through the noise of the party, told him that the police had hypnotized him in an effort to obtain information about that night. When I asked, the man told me that he never did call the cops and tell them they had hypnotized the wrong guy. Furthermore, his conversation with me was the first time he had talked about that night in two decades.

That left me with the other man Claudia thought might have some information, but he was serving a sentence in an unknown provincial corrections facility, so I did as I have always done and wrote the man a letter requesting permission to visit, and sent it to BC Corrections, Adult Custody Division where they would forward it to the appropriate facility. The warden there would then decide whether to give it to the inmate. If he got my letter, I rated my chances of seeing him as slim to none, but if you don't ask, you'll never know. He didn't contact me, but when he was released I received a tip that he regularly attended an Aboriginal friendship centre in Vancouver's Downtown Eastside. When I arrived there I was told I had just missed him. The helpful individual I was speaking with suggested we go outside and see if we could spot him on the sidewalk. The man I was looking for was a block away, waiting for the light to change so he could cross Hastings. Once across the busy street, he disappeared behind some buildings. I got in my car, made a U-turn and drove past him, parking down the street and leaning on the trunk of the car until he reached me. Sadly, after our discussion, this potential suspect/witness proved uncooperative.

I would now consider the option of attempting to surreptitiously obtain a sample of my primary suspect's DNA in the hope the RCMP had DNA from the crime scene on file. This man came to me through extensive interviews with Alberta's sister, Claudia. However, this didn't preclude me from working the case the old-fashioned way, the boring and unromantic method of walking the streets, knocking on doors and talking to anyone who would listen. I knew if I kept asking someone would give me the information I was looking for, and soon I had a home address and vehicle description for this suspect, who by now knew I had been asking around about him. I suspect this is the reason he eventually moved out of town. I kept asking and soon I had his new address. Like American boxer Joe Louis once said: "He can run, but he can't hide."

In July 2001, as a result of a Freedom of Information request, the RCMP advised that the cost of individual E-PANA investigations was not recorded, so I took their lead and didn't keep track of how much money I spent hunting for this guy's DNA. Not because I'm afraid the knowledge of my spending might be used by victims' families to compare my efforts to other investigations, but because it's too damn depressing. I didn't have the resources to conduct a multi-week full-scale surveillance operation on this potential suspect, so I've carried out shorter one- to three-day surveillance operations. I've lurked in restaurants, on-board ferries, and once, attended what was billed an all-Native sporting event where I had been told I would find my man in attendance. Accompanied by my wife, who at the time was also a licenced PI, I headed into the venue. Once inside, a quick look around told me that as expected, the majority of spectators were Aboriginal. My wife and I are not, and we stood out like sore thumbs. As had been my experience working in Aboriginal communities, everyone we encountered was polite and very friendly. Nonetheless, sometimes in this job you feel and look like an outsider, an impression I often got when working in countries like Nicaragua and Costa Rica. Now I know how others might feel right here in their own country.

My suspect never showed up, but I continue to work this case when I can. At every possible opportunity I lurk in this man's shadow, waiting to pounce on his DNA.

Not unlike many of the other Tears cases I've investigated, the information I've gathered on this particular person is just too compelling to dismiss. And, like all the other cases, I hope I'll find more information behind the next door I knock on, from the strangers I stop and talk to on the street or from someone close to the case who has a change of heart and miraculously remembers something new and relevant to the case. So I continue forward with the same stubborn obsession I started with, because from my experience, not just on these cases but from other non-related ones I've investigated over the years, I know this bull-headed attitude often brings on success.

———

The RCMP have only acknowledged that a number of people had come to their attention through the course of their Alberta Williams investigation but would not specifically say how many. They did say over 200 tips had surfaced; some people had been eliminated as possible suspects, while others had not. In order to protect the integrity of their ongoing investigation, the police refused to release any evidence regarding the cause of death or specific details of the case, stating that murder investigations remain active until solved.[2]

That said, the police have told Claudia they were ninety-nine percent sure they knew who Alberta's killer was, but nearly three decades later they have not arrested or charged anyone for Alberta's murder and no one in Claudia's family have ever been invited to one of the RCMP's meetings with the other Tears victim's families.

13. THE SERIOUS CRIME BUNKER

"He means well is useless unless he does well."—Titus Maccius Plautus

Shockingly very little has been reported in the media about the disappearance of nineteen-year-old Lana Derrick. The teenager vanished on October 7, 1995 in the middle of the night from Terrace, BC. Lana, who was a forestry student at a college in Houston, BC, was at home in Thornhill for the Thanksgiving weekend. She went missing after leaving a friend's home at approximately 3:30 a.m.[1] My research in 300-plus Canadian publications found that there was only one mention of her disappearance that year.[2]

On December 5, Terrace RCMP Corporal Rob McKay told the *Vancouver Sun* that because Lana, who had last been seen that early October 7 morning, hadn't checked in with her family, her disappearance was considered very suspicious. Although they wouldn't say if there was a link between her case and others, he was quoted as saying: "If you want to say they were all young Native girls, you could say that, if you want to say these matters all happened in the northern or northwestern region of the province, you could say that, but, really, that's pretty generic to try to link something like this together."

By April 2006 I had managed to come up with a list of Lana Derrick's teachers and classmates from the Natural Resources Forestry Program where she had been enrolled, including a few male students she had been spending a lot of time with. I found the relationships with the male students particularly interesting because they seemed to make her boyfriend jealous. In fact, Constable Liz Douglas, the lead investigator on the case, said Lana had threats from an old boyfriend and Lana's current boyfriend at the time killed himself the night she disappeared.[4] Unfortunately, my investigation of her classmates turned out to be another dead end.

In 2008, I discovered there was one newspaper article about Lana's case published in 1996. It appeared in a Vancouver paper. No stories about Lana appeared in Terrace or any other northern newspaper along the Highway of Tears. This one story was written after RCMP investigators told the media they had called in Dr. Lee Pulos, a Vancouver psychologist, to hypnotize a witness. This person had seen Lana with two men. One was described as Native, approximately thirty years old, with a large stomach, wearing a biker-style leather jacket. The other was tall, skinny, with a pale complexion, long arms and messy looking hair. They were in a blue or grey four-door car with a scrape on the driver's side and a pair of white balls hanging from the rear-view mirror. As a result, composite sketches of two males who were seen getting into a car with Lana in Terrace appeared in *The Province* in Vancouver —a paper published a fifteen-hour drive (or 1,300 kilometres) northeast of the crime scene. Unfortunately, potential witnesses living in Northern BC—who lived in the area where the crime occurred but didn't get the newspaper—would have most likely not seen the sketches. This was a poor use of the media by police.

Sergeant Anders Udsen, the Mountie in charge of the Terrace RCMP's two-person plainclothes investigation section, told the media he believed the answers to the disappearance were likely buried in one of two battered green filing cabinets bearing Lana's name in the detachment's Serious Crime Bunker. These cabinets are full of tips about Lana's disappearance, which police get to when they have time. He said Constable Liz Douglas, the lead investigator on the case, was confident it could be solved and there were a number of leads, but she was needed for "more recent and pressing investigations." Constable Douglas said she never personally knew the missing girl, but Lana had become someone she thought of as a sister. Her boss said "they were just not in a position to provide what's needed to get the job done." His investigators were run off their feet, working more overtime than they could possibly use. Constable Mike Herchuck, the media liaison for Prince George RCMP, also told the media: "If resources were made available and funds, we'd throw them into these investigations." He added:

"In many cases, we just don't have the manpower or the money available to take it to the extra step." Lana's father said he thought the police try very hard but are very much restricted in terms of what they can do in the northwest.[6]

In the fall of 2008, the composite sketches were finally published in Northern British Columbia newspapers. As a result I immediately started to receive tips about possible matches. Within days, two important ones landed in my lap: one tipster gave the name and hometown of an individual who apparently looked almost identical to one of the composites; another tipster identified the other man and provided two possible addresses. I located a picture of one of the men on the Internet. The caller was right: the composite sketch was a close match. I believed both leads worthy of the RCMP's attention, so I passed on the information. Unfortunately, I don't know if the men are viable suspects because they have never been charged and, as was the case with other information I've passed along, I've never heard back from the RCMP either way.

You'd think I would have got the hint by now: "Don't call us, because we're definitely not calling you."

14. CA-CHING

*"Many of white man's ways are past our understanding.
They put great store upon writing; there is always a paper."*
— Four Guns, Oglala Sioux Lakota Chief

It's 2010, not one of the nine murdered and missing women cases along the Highway of Tears has been solved, nor have any of the additional nine cases the RCMP Project E-PANA are investigating in Northern BC. The Native Women's Association of Canada now have a data base of 582 cases of murdered and missing women across Canada. About fifty-four percent of all these occurred in BC and Alberta; twenty-nine percent of the cases occurred in Manitoba, Ontario and Quebec, with the remainder throughout the various other regions of Canada.

In January 2010, almost everyone in BC, including non-sports fanatics, were focused on the upcoming Olympic Games in Vancouver. They would showcase Canada's finest athletes to the world, but what the world didn't see was what was happening up north. Despite all the lights, camera, bureaucracy—and the $900-million price tag for the Games, it was same old same old for the victims and their families along the Highway of Tears.

Ed John, Grand Chief of the First Nations Summit and former Minister for Children and Families, took part in the Olympic

Torch run on Highway 16, telling the media he had been given a choice of carrying the flame in either Vancouver or Prince George. Choosing Prince George allowed him an opportunity to "mark the significance of the flame's journey" along Highway 16.[1] However, Paul Mitchell, Director of the First Nations Centre at the University of Northern BC, had this take on the Olympics: "Something is askew when billions of dollars are being spent to welcome the world to the Olympics when the murdered and missing women's cases remain unsolved and the violence continues."[2]

Three years' earlier, in BC, Robert William Pickton had been convicted of murdering six women while the charges against him for the death of twenty others were stayed by Crown Council. At a price tag of $124 million his investigation has been described as the largest police investigation of any serial killer in Canadian history. Remarkably, some of the costs included purchasing cigarettes; chocolates; a college course; a Christmas present; dental work; a whale tour; and tickets to the Royal BC Museum for witnesses.[3]

What was unknown in 2010 and equally as remarkable would be the revelations disclosed by members of the RCMP two years later, about their organization and investigative prowess—or lack thereof—that surfaced as a result of the Government of British Columbia's Missing Women Commission Inquiry. The inquiry was established by the Lieutenant Governor of BC. It had several goals: inquire into and make findings of fact regarding BC police investigations into the women missing from Vancouver's Downtown Eastside between January 23, 1997 and February 2, 2002; inquire and make findings of fact regarding the January 27, 1998 decision by the Criminal Justice Branch to enter a stay of proceedings on charges against Robert William Pickton of attempted murder, assault with a weapon, forcible confinement and aggravated assault; recommend changes regarding the initiation and conduct of police investigations in BC of missing women and suspected multiple homicides; and recommend changes respecting how homicide investigations in BC by more than one police force were conducted and co-ordinated.[4] During this 2012 Inquiry, retired RCMP Inspector Don Adam described the RCMP as a "big giant bureaucracy" which didn't "actually get down to care sometimes about what's happening to the humans at the bottom, and that's wrong." Obviously, this isn't the image the RCMP wants out there. Nor would they like us to know that in 2012, Deputy Commissioner Gary Bass told the inquiry that as far back as the 1990s there was a "serious deficiency in the investigations of homicides," or that they believed at that time there were 1,800 missing persons in BC. And while the possibility may have lurked in the back of our minds that there was or is one serial killer working in Vancouver's Downtown Eastside or along the Highway of Tears, but not for the inquiry we would not have learned that the RCMP suspected there were more than three serial killers operating in BC at the same time.[5]

During the inquiry, Bass, the man who was once in charge of the RCMP "E" Division Headquarters Major Crime Section,[6] acknowledged that the names Ramona Wilson, Delphine Nikal and Roxanne Thiara had been mentioned within the RCMP, but he didn't know if they were found on Highway 16 and that he "didn't know anything about the cases."[7]

Before this Missing Women Commission of Inquiry got off the ground, Native people in Northern BC were complaining that it didn't include Highway of Tears cases. As a result, the Union of BC Indian Chiefs wrote a formal letter complaining about a "serious perception of conflict of interest" regarding the inquiry's head, Mr. Wally Oppal. The letter pointed out that as attorney general of BC, Mr. Oppal had earlier stated that "he saw no need for an inquiry." The Chiefs also pointed out he was also "part of discussions not to proceed with a trial on twenty of the twenty-six murder charges Pickton faced."[8] David Eby, then director of the BC Civil Liberties Association, thought Oppal was too close to both Crown prosecutors and the government. Carole James, then leader of the BC NDP Party, said he was "too close to the Liberal party."[9]

Perhaps it was this criticism that led to the March 3, 2011 announcement that there would be a Pre-Hearing Conference in

Prince George, in addition to seven Northern Community Forums, held by the inquiry commissioner. But this news didn't discourage further criticism. Chief Jackie Thomas of the Saik'uz First Nation near Vanderhoof said she thought the commission was more interested in "red washing" and "palatable answers" than in a full and open inquiry. She also said she had the impression that the commission was more interested in the optics of consulting with First Nations leaders than in actually meeting with victims' families. As a result, it was not welcome in her community.[10]

The purpose of the forums in Northern BC was said "to gather information about, and suggestions for the improvement of, the investigation and missing and murdered women" in Northern BC. This gathering of information was considered necessary by Commissioner Wally Oppal to make "recommendations for the initiation and investigation of cases of missing and murdered women that are relevant to the province as a whole." Following the informal hearings, he would develop "practical, workable and effective" policy recommendations. I couldn't help but wonder if there was an official template for these kinds of reports, because a few years' earlier, Don Sabo, the author of the *Highway of Tears Recommendation Report*, said that report's purpose was to "present all realistic and achievable Highway of Tears Symposium recommendations."[11]

No matter. On January 21, 2011, the commission held the Pre-Hearing Conference in Prince George, as well as the seven Northern Community Forums. Approximately 400 people attended in Prince George, including the forums in the Highway of Tears communities of Prince Rupert, Gitanyow, Moricetown, Smithers, Hazelton and two in Terrace. The final consultation report was issued a month later: *Standing Together and Moving Forward.*

Some might argue that once you've read the disclaimer on page one there's no reason to read any further. There are phrases such as "represents the views expressed by participants" and warnings that "the commission has not verified any of the facts contained in this report; the content of the report does not necessarily reflect the views of the commissioner and commission staff" and "no conclusions have been reached to date on the issues raised in this report."[12]

That said, the report does touch on a number of Highway of Tears "hot button" issues, including geography, colonialism, residential schools, poverty, discrimination, racism, violence and unhealthy lifestyles. In the first twenty-two pages the RCMP is mentioned just slightly less than forty times; one-third of these references occur in the section called "Recommendations for Moving Forward."

In some ways, this new report's suggestions were as far-fetched as many of those in the 2006 *Highway of Tears Symposium Report.* It noted, for instance: "Things need to change and that change

involves working with each other, the RCMP and governments."
In the old days, you may have found a handful of off-duty RCMP
members willing to play sports with Aboriginal youth, but in today's
culture something like this would be rare indeed. However, this
commission report noted that what is really needed is more police
training, along with good communication, increased staffing, longer
police postings in one location, the creation of a special unit to deal
with missing men and women and serial killers, Amber Alerts and
roadblocks to aid in finding missing persons and suspects, better
databases and fast-tracked DNA testing.

Included in the section "Victim Prevention" were a number
of recommendations made to prevent young women from being
targeted by predators. Everything from essential health and
social services that make sure homes in communities are safe, to
programs that promote equality, education and awareness, as well
as workshops and safe transportation. Community participation
was encouraged via what was described as a "shadowing approach
to the Highway 16 dangers." If people are observed on Highway
16, there should be a community system to get their information
and have someone pick them up and take them where they need
to go. Sounds like a free version of Uber.[13] There was also the
recommendation that when a community member sees a young
person hitchhiking, that person should stop and tell the youth they

will be checking back on them in a week. Seriously, what are the chances of that "feel good" approach ever happening? The stark reality is that had this recommendation been in place years earlier, it would have been of no value to any of the Highway of Tears victims.

After hearing from seventy-nine witnesses over a ninety-two-day period, Mr. Oppal's final report, *Forsaken*, was released before Christmas 2012. Oppal told a press conference that "in many cases what was not done during the missing women's investigations was simply incomprehensible." As examples he noted there was a "systemic bias" in police response to women that went missing and because they were poor, addicted, vulnerable, and Aboriginal, they did not receive equal treatment from the police.[14] The 1,400-plus-page report contained sixty-three recommendations, including a section dedicated to "Critical Police Failures," and their "Underlying Causes." The report concluded with recommendations to improve missing person policies, enhance police investigations and increase police accountability to communities.[15] The cost to taxpayers was $10 million. Included in that total was $839,535 in remuneration to the inquiry's commissioner; $900,656 in compensation to the commission's counsel; $951,630 in remuneration to the commission's associate counsel; and $668,665 in payment to the executive director.[16]

The same day as the *Forsaken Report* was made public, a BC Ministry of Justice news release called "Government Takes

Immediate Action on Missing Women Report" was issued. It noted that the government would use Commissioner Wally Oppal's report to "appoint a 'champion' to provide advice to government as it implements the recommendations." That "champion" would be the Honourable Steven Point, former Lieutenant Governor of British Columbia. In his new appointment he was to "chair a new advisory committee on the safety and security of vulnerable women. This committee will provide community-based guidance on the report's 63 recommendations and two additional proposals." Steven Point was Canada's first Aboriginal Lieutenant Governor, an appointment in BC that ran from 2007 to 2012. Point was also the chief commissioner of the BC Treaty Commission in 2005, was appointed a BC provincial judge in 1999, and served as a director of the University of British Columbia's Native law program.[17]

Point resigned six months into his new role because litigation had sprung from the Pickton case and, in his role as chair of the advisory committee, "his comments and remarks may well become evidence in the course of the litigation."[18]

Point's remuneration for his role as chair of a committee tasked with ensuring the safety and security of vulnerable women was set out to "a maximum" of $220,000 in fees for the one-year contract, or $16,000 dollars per month, including a maximum of $20,000 to cover various expenses such as travel-related accommodation and meals.[19]

Ca-Ching, Ca-Ching, Ca-Ching! The police investigation of serial killer Robert Willie Pickton; Commissioner Oppal's Missing Women Commission of Inquiry consultation report *Standing Together and Moving Forward*; his final report *Forsaken*; the BC Ministry of Justice news release, "Government Takes Immediate Action on Missing Women Report;" and the BC Government's implementation of Commissioner Oppal's report to "appoint a 'champion'" to provide advice to government as it implements his recommendations. Whatever the intentions, this all sounds a lot more like slot-machine payoffs than realistic, progressive movement toward workable solutions.

15. MR. BIG

"Many of us are under the delusion that the police exist solely to deal with crime and keep us safe. That is to ignore the major focus of many of today's top cops on managing reputation—both of their force and, by default, their careers."
— Heather Brooke, Professor of Journalism, City University London

In 1995 RCMP Corporal Gary Shinkaruk transformed himself into a thug from the underworld, a man involved in murder, dirty money, weapons and drugs. He did this as part of an undercover "Mr. Big" sting operation so he could befriend a murderer's co-conspirator. His role played a part in the conviction of Atif Rafay and Sebastian Burns for the murder of Rafay's mother, father and sister in Bellevue, Washington which occurred in 1994.[1]

By 2012 Shinkaruk had been promoted through the ranks to Inspector. That summer I was surprised when Shinkaruk, the man now in charge of the BC RCMP Major Crime, Special Projects Unit, phoned me with an unexpected invitation to meet with him and two senior members of Project E-PANA. Over time, I have not only become a cynic when it comes to my involvement with the RCMP, but more to the point, I just don't trust them anymore. I was aware at the time that a popular American TV crime series was planning an upcoming show on the Highway of Tears. What I didn't find out until later was that the show's producer had already travelled from New York to see Inspector Shinkaruk and his top E-PANA investigators.

The invitation was cordial, but I was still skeptical. I knew the RCMP would be concerned about their image regarding the Highway of Tears. They saw me as a critic with much more information on the matter than the average person or member of the media, so it made sense they would attempt to get an advance heads-up on what I might be planning to say to the Americans. I was also sure they would first try to get me onside by offering some crumbs. If that didn't work, they could use the information I had given them over the years to put a positive spin on our relationship.

Even though I had never met the man, I liked Gary Shinkaruk, rationalizing that he was probably one of the few I knew who were promoted to inspector these days who actually earned their way there by doing police work. I accepted the invitation. When I arrived at E-PANA's Surrey office, I was escorted to a crowded office. Once behind closed doors, we talked about everything except the real reason I was there. The inspector and seasoned Mr. Big con man really did look more like a criminal than a cop, who by nature, or perhaps by design, came across as unpolished and down-to-earth, not at all like the stereotypical RCMP officers I've encountered.

The RCMP has perfected the "carrot-and-stick" approach in order to get what they want. In my case, the carrot was the invitation to the meeting, which they hoped, I thought, would leave me in awe. The stick was Inspector Shinkaruk's dissatisfaction with a remark I had made in reference to E-PANA's use of the ViCLAS computer program. It was a remark that, to my surprise, became a July 2012 ABC News quote of the week: "They put fifty people in front of computers and hoped that a serial killer would jump out at them." What could I say in my defence? Nothing, so I just smiled sheepishly and shrugged.

As we talked Shinkaruk slouched in his chair, displaying an odd posture for an RCMP inspector. At times he was fidgety, moving around in the chair, crossing and uncrossing his arms. Then I realized what he was doing: mirroring my body language, something masters of rapport-building often do. This is a tool used not only by investigators but great sales professionals. It's a way to non-verbally communicate to the target that they are empathetic, understanding, and especially, trustworthy. I don't think the inspector thought he was being particularly effective because, more than once, he asked if I thought he was bullshitting me.

Part of me wanted to believe our meeting was to move past previous problems and personal issues I'd had with E-PANA, but the investigator prevented me from getting sucked into that delusion. I knew that when someone as inconsequential as me gets personally invited to a meeting hosted by such a high-profile RCMP inspector, there is something sinister going on behind the scenes. So yes, I did think he was bullshitting me, but I never said so.

As the two-hour meeting came to a close, the inspector caught me totally by surprise when he openly wondered if any of the E-PANA cases would ever be solved. An unusual thing for an RCMP inspector in charge of a multimillion-dollar investigation to say to someone he knew could easily pick up the phone and call any number of media outlets. But why would he want me to make that call? I didn't have the answer and I didn't make the call, but a short time later I found out he really had been bullshitting me. He knew long before our meeting that Bobby Jack Fowler, an Oregon State convict who had recently died in prison, had been linked by DNA to the 1974 disappearance and murder of Colleen MacMillen. Colleen was a sixteen-year-old whose body was found near 100 Mile House, a community 300 kilometres south of Prince George. Perhaps the inspector had been baiting me into leaking his unusual off-the-cuff remarks so he could then use the opportunity to discredit me and, more importantly, give the RCMP the chance to take credit for their investigation's success regarding the Fowler link. I don't know.

In September 2012 while travelling north along Highway 97 toward Prince George, the RCMP came on the radio live to announce what was called a "significant development." The statement was about the 1974 disappearance and murder of Colleen MacMillen and the DNA link to her killer, deceased Oregon sex-offender and prison inmate Bobby Jack Fowler. So I pulled off the highway to listen. The inspector in charge of the BC RCMP Major Crime, Special Projects Unit declared that there had been a major development in their E-PANA investigation. He noted that E-PANA began in the fall of 2005 to determine if a serial killer or killers were responsible for murdering women travelling along major BC highways.[2] Craig Callens, Deputy Commissioner in charge of BC, followed the inspector by saying today's announcement was "a milestone in the RCMP's commitment to solving a series of missing and murdered women's investigations in BC." Callens also used the opportunity to explain that "historical cases are referred to as cold cases," further explaining that "as far as the RCMP are concerned, there is no such thing as a cold case."[3] However, he certainly knew the Highway of Tears victims' families along Highway 16 didn't share his view about their enthusiastic handling of cold cases. That's probably why, when later asked about their cold-case investigations, RCMP communications officer Corporal Annie Linteau said Mounties were now pursuing the cold cases vigorously.[4]

———

During the shooting of the US TV show on the Highway of Tears, Inspector Shinkaruk invited its correspondent to join him on a guided

RCMP floatplane tour of Highway 16. They travelled the length of the Highway from Prince George to Prince Rupert and back. It included a stop on Hogsback Lake, south of Vanderhoof, where the group landed on the lake where they were met by other investigators. Thanks to the RCMP, the tour made for some spectacular footage. As for the show itself, the RCMP looked good. Inspector Shinkaruk had certainly orchestrated a major publicity coup.

That said, the chronology of events regarding my meeting with Shinkaruk, the RCMP announcement regarding Fowler and the American TV show raise some interesting questions. Consider: according to the RCMP, on May 03, 2012, the FBI's DNA databases linked Bobby Jack Fowler to the murder of Colleen MacMillen, one of eighteen murdered and missing cases E-PANA was investigating.[5] Although this was not a Highway of Tears case, it was an important development in the RCMP's rather bootless but expensive investigation.

Prior to my meeting with Shinkaruk, the RCMP knew about the DNA match with Fowler, yet the inspector decided to tell me he openly wondered if any of the E-PANA cases would ever be solved. Why? The RCMP also knew that a US TV show was planning to shoot a story about the Highway of Tears. In fact, they gave them a guided tour in the RCMP plane but failed to mention Fowler. In September 2012, after the Americans spent time in Northern BC shooting the show, but prior to it being aired, the RCMP made the announcement about Bobby Jack Fowler.

Immediately after the RCMP's radio news conference I began receiving calls from media outlets across Canada, all wanting to solicit my opinion about what they had said. One senior reporter who had been following the Highway of Tears for some time told me it was upsetting that the RCMP would attempt to credit E-PANA and their current investigators with solving the Colleen MacMillen case, despite the fact that the case had only been broken through an astute investigator's careful handling of DNA decades earlier and, more recently, the re-examination of that DNA by a forensic expert and submission to Interpol.

Although the RCMP didn't specifically say it, many in the media believed they were attempting to convince us American killer Bobby Fowler might be responsible for other cases in Northern BC. Ex-Vancouver City Police detective and profiler Inspector Kim Rossmo, who had been one of the first to predict that a serial killer was active in Vancouver's Downtown Eastside, said he thought it didn't make sense that Fowler would have killed nine Highway of Tears victims between 1989 and 2006, describing the suggestion as "extremely unlikely, almost to the point of impossibility."[6]

In my opinion, the solving of any criminal case is the foremost issue. It doesn't matter whether the murder of Colleen MacMillen was solved by a plainclothes detective or a civilian employee in a white lab coat. What does matter is that Fowler was correctly linked to the murder, even though he was never previously an RCMP suspect. What concerns me here however is the spin, the effort and organization that went into the timing of the RCMP announcements, and the float plane rides and, as we'll see, the politics and rhetoric that was to follow every one of the unsolved cases that stretch back over thirty years.

16. POLITICS AND RHETORIC

*"How smooth must be the language of the whites,
when they can make right look like wrong, and wrong like right."*
— Chief Black Hawk of the Sauk People

Since I became involved with the Highway of Tears I've discovered that everyone impacted by the tragedies shares three emotional experiences: frustration, anger and disappointment. Anger and frustration because many victims have been described as drug addicts and prostitutes who hitchhiked their way to death. Though this is simply not true in every circumstance, the families are unfortunately forced to endure the negative characterization while at the same time feeling frustrated, angry and disappointed by the lack of progress made by police. On the other hand, initial primary investigators were frustrated, angry and disappointed by the lack of resources they were given, believing cases could have been solved before they went cold. Police managers are also frustrated, angry and disappointed because this story just won't go away. Federal and provincial politicians, who seem to be at a loss as to what to do, must also be experiencing the weight of frustration, anger and disappointment. All the meetings, discussions, police-speak—and all the politics and rhetoric—plus all the millions of dollars that have been thrown into the Highway of Tears investigations—all this has failed to solve just one Tears case. There seems to be no closure for victims' families and friends. If we want to know why, a quick look at the politics and rhetoric coming out of the issues should give us some insight.

From the beginning, a number of RCMP investigators said cutbacks were preventing cases from being solved; the extra push needed in the form of resources was denied them.[1] How could this be? Why would senior police management prevent their investigators from taking the extra steps that might be needed to solve cases?

To understand the context of these allegations stemming from within the force, it helps to understand the typical RCMP chain of command or management structure. Retired RCMP Corporal Mike Connor gave evidence at the Missing Women Commission of Inquiry in Vancouver in February 2012. He described how he had a certain chain of command to go through and it would be improper for him to bypass his sergeant and staff sergeant and go directly to his inspector or officer in charge of the detachment. As a result, he would brief his immediate supervisors and it would be up to them whether this information was passed further up the chain of command.[2] And resultantly, how much time and money would be spent addressing that information. Connor explained: "No matter how convinced an investigator is to follow a particular line of investigation, once they make their argument to their supervisor, it is their supervisor's decision to make and not the presenter's position to disagree with them."[3] He also said: "In certain circumstances somebody of superior rank could overrule you, but it's more likely an investigator is going to be taking direction from their direct supervisor, although in certain circumstances you could be overruled by a superior-ranking officer who's not your supervisor."[4] It's the RCMP way of doing things.

Retired inspector Don Adam, who also testified at the Missing Women Commission of Inquiry, said: "Police departments march on their budgets and without money they don't do anything, unlike Napoleon who said an army marches on its stomach, and when both police resources and money are tight, police managers look for ways to cut corners."[5]

If there is any truth to this, investigators were required to request assistance from their immediate supervisor, who may or may not agree and who may or may not pass the request up the chain of command to a superior-ranking officer, who likewise may or may not agree, and so on. If it's also true that when "resources and money are tight police managers look for ways to cut corners," we need to know why.

Now cutting costs and underfunding are not new to RCMP investigations. It was reported that members of the Integrated Child Exploitation Unit (ICE) comprised of RCMP and other municipal police force members in BC were "mentally and emotionally exhausted, working far in excess of their capacity to deliver because they are under-resourced."[6] Furthermore, the RCMP unit responsible for fighting terrorist financing and fundraising asked for 126 people when the unit was set up, but was only allowed to start with 17.[7]

That said, do we now have an answer to the question, how did the RCMP prevent eager Mounties from taking the extra steps that might be needed to solve some of the cases?

To be clear, the Royal Canadian Mounted Police is organized under the authority of the *RCMP Act* and headed by the commissioner, whose position was politicized in 1984, making him a deputy minister of the federal government in power. As such he wears two hats.[8] The result is, the feds control the budget and RCMP management must juggle accordingly, so it's important that the RCMP be cut some slack in this instance.

That brings us to the role of the federal and provincial governments in the Tears debacle. The New Democratic Party (NDP), Liberals and Social Credit have all intermittently been in power in BC since the murder of first Tears victim Monica Ignas in 1974. Between the various ruling feds and these three provincial parties, all failed to act on many of the murdered and missing reports that were issued. There was lots of transition where little took place because each government had its own views and priorities with nothing progressive being done on the Tears cases as a result.

Typically, there were also lots of reports, even if good meaning, but little action, allowing the killings and disappearances to continue and the killers to remain free today. In November 2004 for instance, the Canadian Standing Senate Committee on Human Rights released *A Hard Bed to Lie In: Matrimonial Real Property on Reserve*. It made clear that family wellbeing was at stake because Aboriginal women living on reserves did not have the same rights over property as other women in Canada. The committee noted that Aboriginal women on reserves "face unfair and unconstitutional discrimination in the exercise of a right that has profound effects on everyday life, the right to a fair share of the matrimonial property on the breakup of their marriage or common-law relationship." This situation led to many cases that are analogous to that of women forced to leave their country of origin with nothing but hope. While other women may go before the courts to have their rights protected, Aboriginal women living on reserves did not even have that option with respect to the family home. Incredibly, it took until 2013 for this to change with legislation called the *Family Homes on Reserves and Matrimonial Interests or Rights Act*.[9]

The Senate committee said it heard stories about women who had been thrown out of the family home and were forced to leave the reserve with their children with only the clothes on their backs. The situation was described as "morally wrong" and in contravention of equality rights which are guaranteed to everyone in Canada under the *Charter of Rights and Freedoms*. In the committee's opinion, it contravened the rights guaranteed under Section 35 of the Constitution Act of 1982. Furthermore, United Nations treaty bodies have told Canada that this sad reality was incompatible with its international obligations.[10] So now mainstream Canada knows that many women left their reserves with little but the bleakest prospects. And too often these women became the most vulnerable and easily exploitable women in the country.

The Report on the Violence in the Lives of Sexually Exploited Youth and Adult Sex Workers in BC (2006) details more disturbing information about how Aboriginal women are and have been treated in Canadian homes and communities. Research indicated that the vast majority of first experiences of violence and sexual exploitation happened at home during childhood. Many of the adult abusers were authority figures. As such, this situation caused "an extreme degree of silence and shame for those involved." To make matters worse, those who have spoken out against abusers—a sibling, parent, grandparent or local community leaders—have been "blamed and ostracized for breaking the silence."[11] Outside the home, it has been conservatively estimated that at least 800 people are trafficked into Canada each year, and 1,500 to 2,200 people are trafficked through Canada to the United States. The majority of the world's trafficked people are women and girls.[12] Abused runaways or impoverished women from reserves can be especially vulnerable to such horrors, which may account for some of the missing women statistics. God knows still.

More recently, in November 2013, Mary Ellen Turpel-Lafond, BC Representative for Children and Youth, noted that nearly $35 million was spent in meetings discussing Regional Aboriginal Authorities, including large expenditures for running meetings, for consultants to facilitate those meetings, and for producing materials of questionable practical value following said meetings. The materials almost never addressed the actual difficulties children and youth experienced—issues such as parental addictions, domestic violence, poverty, neglect and the need for mental health services or special needs supports. While the government publicly applauded the success of these talks, there was little or no evaluation of what was actually achieved, and limited financial controls subsequently put in place.[13]

The following year the BC Provincial Office of Domestic Violence released a three-year, $5.5 million *Domestic Violence Plan* with a commitment to spend $70 million annually to support survivors of crime, including those fleeing domestic violence. The document indicated that the Ministry of Justice contributes more than $40 million to programs and services for victims of crime including women and children impacted by violence, with Aboriginal women almost three times more likely than non-Aboriginal women to report having been a victim of violent crime.[14]

The Native Women's Association of Canada's (NWAC) *Fact Sheet: Violence Against Aboriginal Women*[15] helps shed further light on the issue. Their report indicates that "nearly one-quarter of Aboriginal women experienced some form of spousal violence" in the five years preceding Statistics Canada's 2004 General Social Survey. Fifty-four percent of Aboriginal women reported "more severe forms of family violence, such as being beaten, being choked, having a gun or knife used against them, or being sexually assaulted." The fact sheet also indicates that government statistics are based on "police-collected data." The majority of this data is collected by the RCMP, which covers "seventy-five percent of Canada's geography and serves more than 650 Aboriginal communities." The data only covers those incidents that are reported to police, and it's believed six out of ten go unreported. These themes would be echoed years later when BC Premier Christie Clark signed an agreement with the First Nations Summit, the Union of BC Indian Chiefs, the BC Assembly of First Nations, and Métis Nation BC in which they all recognized that Aboriginal women and girls suffer disproportionately high levels of violence—and that this violence was rooted in what was described as years of "colonial policies and practices that sought to exclude

Aboriginal people economically and socially, and attempted to destroy their culture."[16]

In February 2014 the Government of BC tabled Bill 3—*Missing Persons Act.* The act gives more power to the police to collect information during missing persons cases, enabling them to enter a private home without a court order if they believe a "minor or vulnerable person is at risk." The BC Civil Liberties Association labelled the bill flawed because information collected to help find missing persons could later be used in criminal proceedings.[17] The Information and Privacy Commissioner for the province was critical of the bill as well because it authorizes expedited access without providing sufficient transparency and oversight.[18] Bill 3 passed the third reading in March 2014.

If we start considering all these political and organizational voices, it seems that the beacon has in fact turned toward issues directly related to missing and murdered Aboriginal women in Canada. Indeed, in May 2014 the RCMP acknowledged there are an astonishing "1,186 police-recorded incidents of Aboriginal homicides and unsolved missing-women investigations." Prime Minister Stephen Harper at that time acknowledged there were forty studies dealing with the issue. "Our government," he said, "from the very outset has set as one of its priorities—one of its most important priorities—tackling crime including violence against women and girls." Roxanne James, then parliamentary secretary to Minister of Public Safety Steven Blaney said: "Let me be clear: Now is not the time for another study." According to Ms. James, now is "the time to take real action and move forward with concrete measures to end violence." To do that, James argued her government had "taken over thirty measures since coming into office," citing two separate $25-million initiatives from the 2010 and 2014 budgets, one of them being a DNA-based missing persons index.[19]

In light of all the results, conclusions and recommendations from all the reports and studies and inquiries and political posturing, I certainly don't believe that the RCMP is responsible for the Highway of Tears tragedies. Rather, they were one of the last in a long line of organizations forced to deal with the realities that make up the Tears cases. I also do not believe in the *Highway of Tears Symposium Recommendation Report*'s oversimplification of the problem that suggests hitchhiking was cause of the tragedies because there was no public transportation alternative along the entire length of Highway 16.[20] Yes, the lack of public transportation is an issue, and solving that problem might help, but it's simply a band-aid solution. All one has to do is look at cities in Lower Mainland BC, where there is an abundance of public transportation. Here transit has not appeared to have made any appreciable change in crime. Furthermore, although lots of studies point out that a lack of transportation is a problem—and rightly so—unless a 24/7 transportation system is implemented with frequent stops at every small town and city along the 700-kilometre Highway of Tears, people will still need to travel from point A to B when transit is not convenient. Yes, transit is an issue but I don't think you can blame a lack of transit for the majority of missing and murdered women cases across Canada. All these studies show that there are many legal, social-economic, race and gender-based issues that place Aboriginal women and girls in highly vulnerable positions. Some are well known to mainstream society, others not so much if at all. But all said and done, the problem remains: none of the information provided by the countless studies has solved the number and frequency of murdered and missing Aboriginal women and girls across country, nor has it led to one solved case along the Highway of Tears.

———

The phone calls I continue to receive are not just from people with tips and information about the Highway of Tears tragedy. Many come from people with stories about physical, mental and sexual abuse and police indifference, people who struggle with feelings that no one cares. Often it appears that these stories just need to be told to someone with a sympathetic ear and the patience to listen. And, just when I begin to believe they'll stop because I think I've heard them all, the telephone rings with another story, often more sad and depressing than the previous one.

I have met hundreds of helpful people along the way, many of whom have become friends. Unfortunately, from time to time I too feel their frustration, anger and disappointment, in part because I haven't solved one of the Tears cases myself and am haunted by the possibility that the information I do pass on to police falls on deaf ears. For example, I gave the Mounties highly time-sensitive information I had obtained regarding an individual who may have been involved in one of the Tears cases, only to later learn it took six months before that information was ever passed on to an investigator. This gives me an idea of what likely happened to the non-time-sensitive information I've passed along. As a result I've asked myself many times over, why bother?

The reality is that far too often, there is very little I can do to help. Perhaps Don Adam, retired RCMP inspector and former head of the Missing Women Task Force, said it best in his letter to the *Vancouver Sun*: "Organizations, governments, the courts are designed to wait for answers, often for years. People aren't."

So what's next? Former Prime Minister Stephen Harper emphatically refused a national inquiry, believing murdered and missing women's cases are not a sociological phenomenon, only crimes to be solved by police.[21/22]

In March of 2015, Ontario Premier Kathleen Wynne said she thought it outrageous Harper did not believe there was a systemic component to the problem. Amnesty Canada said fifty-eight reports have been issued on the issue of "violence against Indigenous women" over the past twenty years. Those reports have resulted in more than 700 recommendations, yet according to Amnesty Canada, "only a handful has been fully implemented."[23] As a province, and as a country, we don't seem to get the message. Instead we're chasing our tails creating reports that initiate little action. Report after report we're running in circles, unable to solve even one Tears case let alone heal the root causes. A highly sympathetic person might suggest all these problems and all these horrible tragedies are way beyond our control; a much less sympathetic and cynical person might suggest that all this has been good for business.

For years I believed that the British Columbia experience regarding murdered and missing Aboriginal women and their treatment by police has mirrored the larger Canadian experience, but I had no proof. Thanks to the media, Canadian's have now finally started to hear about these cases across the country, and we're also learning what retired RCMP Inspector Don Adam learned a long time ago: "You shouldn't have to do an investigation into finding out a simple thing like who's missing."[24]

In fall of 2015 Mr. Harper's Conservatives fell from favour when Canadians overwhelmingly voted in Justin Trudeau's Liberals whose platform included a promise to initiate a national inquiry into murdered and missing Aboriginal women across Canada. When the election dust settled Canadians had also elected ten Native MPs to the House of Commons who represented ridings from coast to coast to coast. Eight of those MPs were Liberals. All eight have stories to share, but perhaps one of the most incredible is Jody Wilson-Raybould's, Canada's new Minister of Justice and Attorney General. Her story is not astonishing because she is an Indigenous female, or because she served as a regional chief for the Assembly of First Nations, has been credited as a founding member of the Indigenous Bar Association of Canada or was a former British Columbia Crown prosecutor. What is incredible is that when she was just a child, her father Bill Wilson, a First Nations leader, told then Prime Minister Pierre Elliott Trudeau about his two daughters. He said that they not only wanted to become lawyers but one day wanted to become Prime Minister. Without a second thought, the Prime Minister told Bill Wilson he would "stick around" until they were ready. Pierre Elliott Trudeau passed away on September 28, 2000. His son now serves witness as the new prime minister.

On Remembrance Day 2015 I received a message from a woman requesting I call her regarding some information she wanted to share. As her voice started to break, she finished by saying: "Having a really hard time finding somebody to listen to me about what I know about the Highway of Tears." It seems the new Liberal Government has been listening, but it remains to be seen if they will be able to carry through on their promises. Mr. Trudeau said he wants an inquiry, but where will he go with that? He has already sent representatives across the country looking for input from a multitude of very different special interest groups, all with distinctly different demands. I hope at the end of the proposed inquiry we're still not chasing our tails, looking for answers. More importantly, I hope we find practical, workable, and achievable solutions that will make a difference. We owe that to the victims, their families—and to all of us.

17. NORMAN

"The circle, like the Dream Hoop, brings us ever back to where we start."
— Luther Standing Bear, Oglala Sioux, 1868-1937

I was beat. I had been on the road sixteen-hours working my way from Vancouver through Prince George to Smithers. I had a quick bite and went to my motel for the night. I had chosen this room because of its location, which made it easy for me to keep an eye on my car and anyone prowling around outside. I had been asking about some rough characters and was feeling particularly wary. No matter. I fell into bed still obsessing over the day's dismal results and my lack of progress.

At 3:00 a.m. I was awakened from my fitful sleep by someone knocking on the door. I jumped out of bed, went over to the window and slowly moved one corner of the curtain aside, peering out into the night to see who was there. The parking lot was quiet, but there was a shadowy male figure standing just to the right of the door.

"What do you want?" I shouted.

"To talk to you!" The man looked at the bottom of the door ... and knocked again.

"Who are you?" I snapped, looking to see if he was alone.

"I want to talk about the Highway of Tears."

"What's your name?"

"I want to talk about the Highway of Tears."

"What's your name?"

"Norman."

"Norman who?"

"Norman!"

How did he find me? As always, I conducted counter-surveillance earlier that night to make sure I wasn't followed. For me, counter-surveillance involves spending at least fifteen to twenty minutes driving around, systematically glancing over my shoulder to determine if someone is on my trail. Once convinced I'm clear, I carry on to my destination. So Norman shouldn't have happened.

I scoured the motel parking lot for anyone who may have accompanied the man to my room. Then, as if reading my mind, he said in monotone, "I'm alone."

Unlike television's portrayal of private investigators, it's illegal for PIs in Canada to carry a firearm. In the province of BC, it's also illegal to possess restraining devices or any other items that may be used to control a suspect, even if those things are perfectly legal for members of the public to possess. It was the middle of the night and I was off duty, so to speak. So I yanked on a pair of pants and from the nightstand grabbed my large knife, collapsible baton and bear spray which I then strapped to my belt. I looked out the window one more time before carefully turning the knob. As I slowly opened the door I stood off to the side and slightly behind it, using the toes and heel of my right foot as a door stop just in case I had to slow or stop my visitor and anyone else who might want to storm the room.

Norman appeared to be alone so I reluctantly let him inside, closing the door and locking it with the deadbolt so no one else could follow.

Almost immediately after the door was closed Norman told me that he knew who I was and wanted to confess to several of the murders.

"How did you find me?" I asked.

He ignored my question. "I'll show you, I'll show you!" he exclaimed. He then said he wanted to take me to the women's graveyard, to show me where all his victims were buried.

When I suggested that we call the RCMP first, his only comment was: "Later."

"You said you were Norman, is that right?"

"Yeah, Norman."

"Norman, I'm Ray."

"I know," he mumbled.

Before we left the room I apologized for the fact that I had to search him for weapons. His only response was: "I know."

We went outside and got in my car while I scanned the parking lot for anything suspicious. Other than a scruffy cat, we were alone. As we left, Norman told me to drive east. I did, but I took the first right instead.

"What … what's going on?" He started to panic.

"I'm just making sure no one is following us."

"Following us … Who's following us?" He sounded surprised.

"Hopefully no one, Norman."

More counter-surveillance. Then I turned back to Highway 16 and east through the moonlit countryside. As I drove Norman quietly and without emotion confessed to several murders. His words were captured on my hidden tape recorder. After what seemed like hours but was probably only twenty minutes, Norman told me to slow down and pull off the highway onto a dirt trail that ran north, out of sight into the bush. We sat speechless like two shadows in the moonlight as I slowly drove the trail. What was I thinking? There was no cellphone service and I was with a psychopath who was also the only person in the world who knew where I was. Thirty minutes passed before Norman told me to pull over and stop. I turned the car off the trail as much as I could and parked beside a barbwire fence, at the foot of a small ridge, west of the little lake we had just past.

"Them girls are up there." Norman casually pointed to the top of a ridge.

I slowly followed him through a ditch. We climbed the fence and started walking up the hill on a small animal trail through the grass. Norman occasionally looked back to make sure I was still following him; I occasionally looked back to make sure no one was following me. Once on top of the ridge, Norman pointed to nine grass-covered mounds of dirt, some timeworn and others less aged by Mother Nature. He walked over to a mound of fresh dirt, got down on his hands and knees, and began pulling the dirt aside with his bare hands. In a few minutes, he started tugging at some orange plastic. Before I had time to fully comprehend what was happening, he raised his arm to show me a skull precariously balancing on his open palm. Once he was sure I saw it, he quickly returned it and covered up the hole with soil.

I pulled out my GPS and recorded our location. The moon had left the morning sky as the sun began to brighten the eastern horizon.

"You know we have to go to the RCMP?" I said.

Still looking down at the mound, Norman nodded. "I know."

We got back in the car, made a U-turn on the narrow trail, and headed back to Smithers. As we arrived in town, I noticed two police cars at the hotel coffee shop, so I quickly pulled into the parking lot. Without saying anything, we got out of the car and walked in. Three Mounties were having breakfast at a table in a corner at the back. Shadowed by Norman, I approached and introduced myself.

No one at the table said a word. In the most deliberate manner possible I explained that the small man now standing directly behind me, as though to hide himself from the police, was Norman. He had just confessed to the murder of nine Highway of Tears victims, but had also just taken me to his dumpsite and showed me a human skull dug up from a shallow grave. None of them spoke, so I added, "Norman wants to make a formal confession."

The Mountie with the designer sunglasses propped on top of his shaved head put down his coffee cup. "Even if there are nine victims buried where you say, if they are Highway of Tears cases they are not our cases, they're Vancouver's."

"But—"

Before I could finish my sentence, he interrupted. "This has nothing to do with us. You need to talk to Vancouver."

The other two Mounties looked up at me, nodding in agreement.

"But Vancouver is a long way away, and we're in Smithers, as are the bodies," I said.

The cop who'd first spoken took another sip of coffee, then looked up over his cup, acting surprised that I was still standing there. "I told you, this has nothing to do with us, you need to talk to Vancouver."

The three police officers shook their heads, disgusted, and continued eating. There was nothing else to do. Norman and I got back in the car and tried another group of cops we spotted just outside of town, but to no avail. So we drove all over the north for a week, stopping every RCMP member we saw. Nothing. Had Norman's crimes not been so horrendous, I would have dropped him off somewhere and carried on as though we had never met. But we had to carry on. Finally, I received a phone call from Vancouver telling me to go to Smithers detachment so Norman could complete a video interview.

I don't know what happened to Norman afterwards because that's the part of the story when I first woke up shivering, my motel room pillow and bedsheets soaked with sweat. The entire episode marked the beginning of a year-long recurring nightmare. The nightmare started after I took a man claiming to be a witness to Ramona Wilson's murder to Smithers RCMP and was asked: "Who's Ramona Wilson?"

I worry that the only way a Highway of Tears tragedy will ever be solved will be when a murderer walks into an RCMP detachment and confesses. Then again, even if he did, what are the chances he'd be told:

"It's not our case, call Vancouver."

NOTES

INTRODUCTION

1   The Manitoba Historical Society, Historic sites of Manitoba, Birtle Indian Residential School (Birtle) http://www.mhs.mb.ca/docs/sites/birtleresidentialschool.shtml [Accessed 18 Mar 2014]

2   Where the children are website, http://www.lesenfantsdevenus.ca/en/projector/index.php?req=getVideo&language=en&id=21 [Accessed 18 Mar 2014]

3   Truth and Reconciliation Commission of Canada Report: What We Have Learned— Principals of Truth and Reconciliation, page 6.

4   The Record [Kitchener, Ont] 13 Nov 1995: D10.

5   Aboriginal Justice in Saskatchewan 2002-2021: http://www.justice.gov.sk.ca/justicereform/volumeone/14ChapterNine.pdf.

6   Travel writer pans Hwy. 16 - http://www.pgfreepress.com/travel-writer-pans-hwy-16/ [Accessed 30 Sep 2014]

7   Report of the Aboriginal Justice Inquiry of Manitoba: The Deaths of Helen Betty Osborne and John Joseph Harper, Commissioners A.C. Hamilton and C.M. Sinclair, 1991. http://www.ajic.mb.ca/volume.html

8   Trinh Theresa Do, CBC News: RCMP confirm report of more than 1,000 murdered aboriginal women. Aboriginal women make up 4 per cent of population, but 16 per cent of all murdered females. Posted: May 02, 2014 8:55 PM ET | Last Updated: May 02, 2014 10:37 PM ET [Recovered 16 Nov 2014]

9   Human Rights Watch Report: THOSE WHO TAKE US AWAY. Abusive Policing and Failures in Protection of Indigenous Women and Girls in Northern British Columbia, Canada (2013)

CHAPTER 1

1   Carl Fussman, Clint Eastwood: What I've Learned, Esquire, http://www.esquire.com/features/what-ive-learned/clint-eastwood-quotes-0109

2   Royal Canadian Mounted Police Musical Ride: http://www.rcmp-grc.gc.ca/mr-ce/media-eng.htm [Recovered 23 September 2014]

3 | Winnipeg Free Press: Tuesday July 9, 1968

1   Erica Bulman, QMI Agency, Serial killing a west coast phenomenon. Toronto Sun. First posted: Wednesday, October 19, 2011: 01:40 AM EDT: Updated: Wednesday, October 19, 2001: 01:51 AM EDT. [Accessed 01/11/2014]http://www.torontosun.com/2011/10/19/serial-killing-a-west-coast-phenomenon#

2   http://www.mytripjournal.com/travel-397040-prince-george-british-columbia-totem-poles-cocktail-hour-feet-long

3   http://sixsixthreethreenorth.blogspot.ca/2010_05_01_archive.html [Recovered 21 February 2016]

4   Indian Residential School Resources. http://irsr.ca/lejac-indian-residential-school/ Indian Residential School Resources - Lejac Indian Residential School—Fraser Lake [Accessed 19 Oct 2014]

5   Yellow Head Highway. http://en.wikipedia.org/wiki/Yellowhead_Highway [Accessed 25 Nov 2011]

6   BC Ministry of Justice, Crime and Police Statistics, http://www.pssg.gov.bc.ca/policeservices/statistics/#crimestats [Accessed 20 Mar 2014]

7   http://www.huffingtonpost.com/diane-dimond/orange-county-serial-killer_b_1222710.html - Is There a Serial Killer Near You? Diane Dimond [Accessed 01/11/20]14

8   http://www.theglobeandmail.com/news/national/the-life-and-death-of-clifford-olson/article4197011/?page=all [30 Sept. 2011]

9   http://www.theglobeandmail.com/news/national/the-life-and-death-of-clifford-olson/article4197011/?page=all [20 Mar 2014]

10 http://www.ctvnews.ca/crown-says-pickton-confessed-to-killing-49-1.225554

11 The Canadian Press. Published Tuesday Nov. 16 2010, 6:50 AM EST

12 Stevie Cameron; On The Farm, Robert William Pickton and the Tragic Story of Vancouver's Missing Women; Pg. 37.

13 R.J. Williams, Isns. OIC Major Crime North, "K" Division, Royal Canadian Mounted Police, Re: Josbury vs. Her Majesty The Queen, (Project Evenhanded) Request for Assistance—External Review, File: 2002E-3220. [2002-11-06] P. 26.

14 https://ca.news.yahoo.com/blogs/dailybrew/b-c-woman-dubbed-serial-killer-waiting-appealing-181059421.html [Recovered 22 July 14]

15 http://www.theglobeandmail.com/news/british-columbia/high-risk-animal-killer-plans-to-live-in-vancouver-public-warned/article7016117/ [Recovered 22 Jul 2014]

16 http://www2.gov.bc.ca/assets/gov/law-crime-and-justice/criminal-justice/police/publications/statistics/2014-police-resources.pdf [27 Feb 2016]

17 Whitehorse Star [Whitehorse, Y.T] 07 Sep 2000: 4.

18 http://www.for.gov.bc.ca/hfp/mountain_pine_beetle/facts.htm [Recovered 04 Nov 2014]

19 Vanderhoof Family History Project: http://www.vanderhoofproject.com/index.php/name

20 http://www.hellobc.com/vanderhoof.aspx [Recovered 20 Mar 2104]

21 http://www2.gov.bc.ca/assets/gov/law-crime-and-justice/criminal-justice/police/publications/statistics/2014-police-resources.pdf [27 Feb 2016]

22   Tony MacGregor, Northern Voice, Sep. 2011: http://www.ufobc.ca/Supernatural/Cropcircles/vanderhoof2e.htm

23   http://www.ufobc.ca/Supernatural/AnimalMutilations/buffalo_v2.htm [Recovered 20 Mar 22014]

24   http://news.nationalpost.com/news/canada/at-least-4000-aboriginal-children-died-in-residential-schools-commission-finds [Recovered 20 February 2016]

25   RCMP News Release, Webmaster "E" Division Communications Section Apr 23rd, 2003 - 09:38:01 AM File #E-Division 1994E-14664 Recovered from http://www.turtleisland.org/discussion/viewtopic.php?f=4&t=642#p812 [Recovered 14 Oct 2011]

26   http://www.hellobc.com/burns-lake.aspx [Recovered 20 Mar 2014]

27   http://tourism.burnslake.ca/ [Recovered 20 Mar 2014]

28   The Wikipedia Website: http://en.wikipedia.org/wiki/Burns_Lake,_British_Columbia [Recovered 14 Jul 2011]

29   http://www2.gov.bc.ca/assets/gov/law-crime-and-justice/criminal-justice/police/publications/statistics/2014-police-resources.pdf [27 Feb 2016]

30   http://www.pssg.gov.bc.ca/policeservices/statistics/docs/2_Bulkley_Nechako.pdf [Recovered 04 Nov 2014]

31   http://www2.gov.bc.ca/assets/gov/law-crime-and-justice/criminal-justice/police/publications/statistics/2014-police-resources.pdf [27 Feb 2016]

32   http://www.bcnorth.ca/magazine/pages/jim/egg/egg1.htm [Recovered 20 Mar 2014]

33   Hall, Neil. Daily News [Prince Rupert, B.C] 13 Dec 2005: 11.

34   http://www2.gov.bc.ca/assets/gov/law-crime-and-justice/criminal-justice/police/publications/statistics/2014-police-resources.pdf [27 Feb 2016]

35   http://www.hellobc.com/terrace.aspx [Recovered 20 Mar 2014]

36   Army Years 1916-1945 Mutiny: http://spcoll.library.uvic.ca/Digit/schoolnet/digicol/pearkes/mutiny.html [Recovered 14 Oct 2011]

37   http://www.kermode-terrace-bc.com/spiritbear.html [Recovered 20 Mar 2014]

38   http://www.hellobc.com/prince-rupert.aspx [Recovered 20 Mar 2014]

39   http://www.pssg.gov.bc.ca/policeservices/statistics/#crimestats [Recovered 04 Nov 2014]

40   http://www.hellobc.com/prince-rupert.aspx [Recovered 20 Mar 2014]

CHAPTER 3

1   Proctor, Jason, The shadow of death: One grieving mother says the only thing that keeps her going is knowing that one day God will judge her daughter's killer: [Final Edition] The Province [Vancouver, B.C] 06 Feb 2000: A16.

2   Union of BC Indian Chiefs website: http://www.ubcic.bc.ca/about/#axzz3E3oZa5ks [Accessed 22 September 2014]

3   http://www.cbc.ca/news/canada/500-gather-at-highway-of-tears-symposium-1.590736 500 gather at 'highway of tears symposium CBC News Posted: Mar 31, 2006 7:45 AM ET | Last Updated: Mar 31, 2006 8:08 AM ET

4   The Vancouver Sun, Vancouver, B.C.: 15 Sep 1990: 8.

5   Kines, Lindsay. The Vancouver Sun, Highway 16 road of death for Indian teenagers: A serial killer is considered a possibility in three slayings and two disappearances: DISAPPEARED: Killings though to be the work of a stranger: [Final Edition] Vancouver, B.C.: 05 Dec 1995: .1.

6   Jason Proctor. The Province. Vancouver, B.C.: Feb 6, 2000. Pg. A. 16

7   http://www.cbc.ca/archives/entry/cameras-cameras-everywhere [Recovered 21 February 2016]

8   Canadian Press NewsWire [Toronto] 27 Mar 1995: n/a [Recovered 21 February 2016

9   Newswire. Times Colonist. Victoria, B.C: Dec 6, 1995. Pg. 1.

10 Clare Ogilvie. The Province. Vancouver, B.C,: Aug 28, 1994. Pg. A.24

11 McDonald, Jonathan. Friend hunts for clues to killer: [Final edition] The Province, Vancouver, B.C.: 05 Sep 1995:

12 The Vancouver Sun [Vancouver, B.C] 29 Aug 1994: B4.

13 Colbourn, John. The Province, Vancouver, B.C.: 13 Dec 1994: 19.

14 Ibid

15 Colburn, John. The Province. Vancouver BC: 13 Dec. 1994: 19.

16 Jiwa Salim. The Province, Vancouver B.C.: 25 Oct 1995:9.

17 Jeremy Deutssch—Williams Lake Tribune—October 23, 2007

18 Dennis Mackay. Hansard, Debates of the Legislative Assembly. Safe Transportation. Monday, November 19, 2007, Morning Sitting, Volume 24, Number 8.

19 Jeremy Deutssch—Williams Lake Tribune—October 23, 2007

20 The City of Quesnel/Unsolved Crimes and Missing Persons—City of Quesnel Web Site - http://www.city.quesnel.bc.ca/RCMP/RCMP-Unsolved.asp—Recovered 2/24/1010

21 Frank Peebles. Alaska Highway News. Fort St. John, B.C. : Nov 27, 2006. Pg. A.3

22 The Highway of Tears Symposium Recommendation Report, June 16, 2006 by when the Lheidi T'enneh Frist Nation, Carrier Sekani Family Services, Carrier Sekani Tribal Council, Prince George Friendship Centre and the Prince George Nechako Aboriginal Employment & Training Association.

23 Neal Hall, Vancouver Sun Dec. 12, 2009 http://www.vancouversun.com/news/Police +reveal+details+Pana+investigation+into+female+unsolved+cases+northern/2331959/ story.html

24 The Windsor Star [Windsor, Ont] 03 Sep 1994: 1.

25 Hatherly, Joanne. Times - Colonist [Victoria, B.C] 02 July 2010: A.4.

26 Bolan, Kim. Alaska Highway News [Fort St. John, B.C] 20 Sep 2011: A.8.

27 Alaska Highway News [Fort St. John, B.C] 23 Jan 2003: A3.

28 Hall, Neal; Kines, Lindsay. The Vancouver Sun [Vancouver, B.C] 16 September 1995: .4.

29 CBC Digital Archives. http://www.cbc.ca/archives/entry/cameras-cameras-everywhere

30 http://www.theguardian.com/world/2016/feb/17/missing-and-murdered-indigenous-women-in-canada-could-number-4000 [Recovered 21 February 2016]

CHAPTER 4

1   Albert Szent-Gyorgyi. BrainyQuote.com, Xplore Inc, 2014. http://www.brainyquote.
    com/quotes/quotes/a/albertszen389956.html, accessed November 6, 2014

2   The Aboriginal Justice Implementation Commission: http://www.ajic.mb.ca/volumeII/
    chapter1.html

3   http://www.ajic.mb.ca/volumeII/chapter1.html [Recovered 26 July 2014]

4   August 13, 1989. Howard Witt, Chicago Tribune. http://articles.chicagotribune.
    com/1989-08-13/news/8901040313_1_canadian-indians-pas-suspects [Recovered 26
    July 2014]

5   http://www.ajic.mb.ca/volumeII/chapter1.html [Recovered 20 Mar 2014]

6   The Aboriginal Justice Implementation Commission http://www.ajic.mb.ca/

7   The Aboriginal Justice Implementation Commission.

8   The INT for Cross-National Academic Research. The Scope of FBIS and BBC Open-Source
    Media Coverage, 1979–2008 (U) https://www.cia.gov/library/center-for-the-study-of-
    intelligence/csi-publications/csi-studies/studies/volume-54-number-1/PDFs-Vol.-54-
    No.1/U-%20Studies%2054no1-FBIS-BBC-Coverage-Web.pdf   [Recovered 20 Mar 2014]

9   The INT for Cross-National Academic Research. The Scope of FBIS and BBC Open-Source
    Media Coverage, 1979–2008 (U) https://www.cia.gov/library/center-for-the-study-of-
    intelligence/csi-publications/csi-studies/studies/volume-54-number-1/PDFs-Vol.-54-
    No.1/U-%20Studies%2054no1-FBIS-BBC-Coverage-Web.pdf   [Recovered 20 Mar 2014]

10 Bronskill, Jim. National Post [Don Mills, Ont] 15 Feb 2002: A4.

11 Huras, ADAM. Edmonton Journal [Edmonton, Alta] 01 Dec 2011: A.17.

13 Huras, Adam. Edmonton Journal [Edmonton, Alta] 01 Dec 2011: A.17.

14 Lindsay Kines, Lori Culbert and Kim Bolan. The Vancouver Sun [Vancouver, B.C] 26 Sep
    2001: A1 / FRONT

15 Lindsay Kines. The Vancouver Sun. Vancouver, B.C.: Dec 5, 1995. Pg. B.1

16 Trick, Bernice. Prince George Citizen [Prince George, B.C] 18 Feb 2006: 13/. [Recovered
    28/10/2011]

17 Lindsay Kines. The Vancouver Sun. Vancouver, B.C.: Dec 5, 1995. Pg. B.1

18 Terrace Standard. Terrace, B.C.: November 1, 2006. Pg 5.

19 http://www.bccrimestoppers.com [Recovered 22 Mar 2014]

20 Terrace Standard. Terrace, B.C.: November 1, 2006. Pg 5.

21 The Prince George Free Press. Prince George, B.C.: Mar 3, 2006. Pg. A.3

22 Eathan Baron, The Province Newspaper, Vancouver, B.C.: Mar 06, 2006.

23 Lakes District News [Burns Lake] 04 Oct 2006: 6.

24 Lakes District News [Burns Lake] 04 Oct 2006: 6.

25 The Interior News [Smithers, B.C] 28 Sep 2006. 1.

26 Lakes District News. Burns Lake, B.C.: Oct 4, 2006, pg. 6

27 The Interior News. Smithers, B.C.: Oct 5, 2006. pg. A.5

28 The Interior News. www.interior-news.com [Recovered 5/16/2007]

29 Jeremy Hainsworth. Trail Times. Trail, B.C.: May 17, 2007. Pg.2

CHAPTER 5

1   Warrior Publications. https://warriorpublications.wordpress.com/2015/07/28/rcmp-pays-out-undisclosedamount-for-horrifying-treatment-of-first-nations-woman-in-saskatchewan/#more-6799

2   Warrior Publications. https://warriorpublications.wordpress.com/2015/01/08/mountie-takes-aboriginalwoman-home-from-jail-cell-to-pursue-relationship/

3   Warrior Publications. https://warriorpublications.wordpress.com/2014/09/26/bands-chief-wants-rcmpapology-for-racist-comments/#more-4697

4   David Steinhart and Herald Graphic. Calgary Herald [Calgary, Alta] 08 Nov 1992: A1/FRONT.

5   Kim Bolan and Chad Skeleton. Times—Colonist [Victoria, B.C] 05 Apr 2006: A3.

6   Potvin, Kevin. Vancouver Courier [Vancouver, B.C] 19 Apr 2006: 11.

7   Ian Mulgrew, Kim Bolan Chad Skelton and Maurice Bridge. The Vancouver Sun [Vancouver, B.C] 13 Apr 2006: A1 Front

8   Lindsay Kines, Lori Culbert and Kim Bolan. B.C. slow to adopt lessons of Bernardo: Police face obstacles tracking down serial predators Series: Missing Women: [Final Edition] The Vancouver Sun [Vancouver, B.C] 26 Sep 2001: A1 / Front

9   Chad Skelton. Daily News. Prince Rupert, B.C.: Oct 3, 2006. Pg. 11

10 Chad Skelton. The Vancouver Sun. Vancouver, B.C.: Oct 5, 2006. Pg. A. 4

11 The Prince George Free Press [Prince George, B.C] 21 Sep 2007: A7.

12 Editorial: Where are the answers about Ian Bush's death? The Globe and Mail, Tuesday, May 9, 2006Published Monday, May. 15 2006, 4:30 PM EDT Last updated Sunday, Apr. 05 2009, 9:07 AM EDT http://www.theglobeandmail.com/news/national/editorial-where-are-the-answers-about-ian-bushs-death/article1099480/ [Accessed 22 Oct 2014]

13 2011BC Civil Liberties Association (BCCLA) released their report titled, "Small Town Justice, A report on the "RCMP in northern and rural BC,"

14 http://www.archives.gov.on.ca/en/e_records/ipperwash/policy_part/research/pdf/Rudin.pdf

15 Mulgrew, Ian. Times-Colonist. Calls grow following Ramsay sentencing: [Final Edition] [Victoria, B.C] o3 June 2004: B3

16 Mulgrew, Ian. the Vancouver Sun [Vancouver, B.C] 03 June 2004: B1 Front.

17 http://www.theglobeandmail.com/news/politics/legal-misstep-lets-catholics-off-hook-for-residential-schools-compensation/article29657424/)

18 The Roman Catholic Diocese of Prince George Web Site: http://www.pgdiocese.bc.ca/our-diocese/parishes/ [Recovered 20 Mar 2014]

19 Vancouver Rape Relied & Women's Shelter Web Site: http://www.rapereliefshelter.bc.ca/learn/resources/canadian-association-sexualassault-centres-response-bishop-oconnor-case [Recovered 20 Mar 2014]

20 Canadian Conference of Catholic Bishops Web Site: http://www.cccb.ca/site/content/view/2503/1062/lang,eng/ [Recovered 20 Mar 2014]

CHAPTER 6

1   Lhedli T'enneh Web Site: http://www.lheidli.ca/ [Recovered 14 Feb 2014]

2   British Columbia, Ministry of Public Safety and Solicitor General News Release. POLICE AND COMMUNITY. TAKE ACTION ON HIGHWAY 16. www2.news.gov. bc.ca/news_releases_2005-2009/2006PSSG0008-000135.htm. 28 Feb 2006 [Accessed 09 Nov 2014]

3   Meissner, Dirk. Canadian Press NewsWire [Toronto] 01 Mar 2006: n/a

4   Meissner, Dirk. Canadian Press NewsWire [Toronto] 01 Mar 2006: n/a

5   http://www.opinion250.com/blog/view/21187/1/instead

6   The Highway of Tears Symposium Recommendation Report. http://www.turtleisland. org/healing/highwayoftears.pdf

7   British Columbia News Release 2006PSSG0010-000310, March 30, 2006

8   Report On The Health Of British Columbians Provincial Health Officer's Annual Report 2001:http://www.health.gov.bc.ca/pho/pdf/phoannual2001.pdf [Recovered 12 June 2016]

9   Victoria Transport Policy Institute: http://www.vtpi.org/soc_ex.pdf [Recovered 05 Apr 2014]

10   http://povertyandhumanrights.org/wp-content/uploads/2009/09/ BCCEDAWopedfinal.pdf

11   Hall, Profile. Daily News [Prince Rupert, B.C] 13 Dec 2005: 11.

12   Meissner, Dirk. The Globe and Mail [Toronto, Ont] 31 Mar 2006: S.3.

13   Daily News [Prince Rupert, B.C] 03 Apr 2006: 1 / Front.

14   The Prince George Free Press. Prince George, B .C.: Mar 29, 2006. Pg. A.1

15   Meissner, Dirk. Tribune [Welland, Ont] 31 Mar 2006: B8

16   Anonymous. The Times - Transcript [Moncton, N.B] 01 Apr 2006: B.10.

17   Meissner, Dirk. Canadian Press NewsWire [Toronto] 31 Mar 2006: n/a.

18   Frank Peebles. Prince George Citizen. Prince George, B.C.: Apr 4, 2006. Pg. 1. Front

19   Peebles, Frank. Prince George Citizen [Prince George, B.C] 04 Apr 2006: 1 / Front. [Recovered 05 Oct 2014]

20   Lakes District News [Burns Lake] 21 June 2006: 9.

21   Hall, Neal. Edmonton Journal [Edmonton, Alta] 22 June 2006: 5.

22   Consultation Report Prepared For The Missing Women Commission of Inquiry February 2012

23   James, Peter. Prince George Citizen [Prince George, B.C] 27 Feb 2014: A.13.

24   The Highway of Tears Symposium Recommendation Report, June 16, 2006 by when the Lheidi T'enneh Frist Nation, Carrier Sekani Family Services, Carrier Sekani Tribal Council, Prince George Friendship Centre and the Prince George Nechako Aboriginal Employment & Training Association.

25   The Interior News [Smithers, B.C] 11 July 2007: 1.

26   Frank Peebles. Prince George Citizen. Prince George, B.C.: Jun 23, 2006. P. 1/Front

27   Peebles, Frank. Dawson Creek Daily News [Dawson Creek, B.C] 18 Oct 2007: 3.

28   The Interior News [Smithers, B.C] 02 Nov 2006: 3

29 The Prince George Free Press. Prince George, B.C.: Mar 30, 2007. Pg. A.28

30 Baker, George T. Daily News [Prince Rupert, B.C] 13 Apr 2009. 2.

31 Peebles, Frank. Prince George Citizen [Prince George, B.C] 31 May 2010: 1.

32 Prince George Citizen. Highway of Tears advocacy earns award for Kellas. [Prince George, B.C] 03 Nov 2014: A.5 [Accessed 05 Nov 2014]

33 Carrier Sekani Family Services Highway of Tears. Preventing Violence against women. http://www.highwayoftears.ca/ [Accessed 09 Nov 2014]

34 Todd Hamilton Managing. The Interior News [Smithers, B.C] 29 June 2006: 4.

CHAPTER 7

1 How police crack open criminal minds - Joe Friesen Published Monday, Jan. 19 2004, 12:00 AM EST. http://www.theglobeandmail.com/news/national/how-police-crack-open-criminal-minds/article992952/ (Recovered 02 August 2014)

2 The Interior News [Smithers, B.C] 05 Oct 2006: A1

3 Public Engines. PublicEngines Launches Crime Data Quality Tools for Law Enforcement. http://www.publicengines.com/company/press/PublicEngines-Launches-Crime-Data-Quality-Tools-for-Law-Enforcement.php [Accessed 10 Nov 2014]

4 The Prince George Free Press. RCMP comments miff investigator [Prince George, B.C] 13 Oct 2006: A7.[Accessed 10 Nov 2014]

5 http://www.rcmp-grc.ca/viclas/viclas-e.htm (Recovered 10/12/2007)

6 RCMP GAZETTE, Vol. 56, No. 10, 1994

7 RCMP Fact Sheets 2000/01 http://dsp-psd.pwgsc.gc.ca/Collection/JS62-70-2001E.pdf (Recovered date Unknown) RCMP Fact Sheets 2000/01, No. 40 (Hard Copy On File)

8 Data Mining and Expert Systems in Law Enforcement Agencies: Volume VIII, No.2, 2007 Issues in Information Systems

9 http://www.rcmp-grc.ca/viclas/viclas-e.htm (Recovered 10/12/2007)

10 RCMP GAZETTE, Vol. 56, No. 10, 1994

11 RCMP GAZETTE, Vol. 69, No. 1, 2007

12 http://www.rcmp-grc.gc.ca/tops-opst/bs-sc/viclas-salvac-eng.htm (Recovered 20/12/2014)

13 http://www.rcmp-grc.gc.ca/tops-opst/bs-sc/viclas-salvac-eng.htm (Recovered 10/12/2014)

14 Computer system credited in murder probe is little used by cops. Canadian Press NewsWire [Toronto] 01 Aug 1996: n/a.

15 Kines, Lindsay. The Vancouver Sun [Vancouver, B.C] 17 June 1998: A7.

16 http://www.rcmp-grc.ca/viclas-e.htm; [RCMP Website], [Retrieved Oct 12, 2007]

17 Government of Canada National Inquiry into Missing and Murdered Indigenous Women and Girls Web Site: http://www.aadnc-aandc.gc.ca/eng/1449240606362/1449240634871

18 http://www.rcmp-grc.gc.ca/tops-opst/viclas-salvac-eng.htm#issues: [Recovered July 24, 2011]

19 Kines, Lindsay. The Vancouver Sun [Vancouver, B.C] 12 May 1999: A7.

20   Lindsay Kines, Lori Culbert and Kim Bolan Special Report: Missing Women: Part Five: The Vancouver Sun [Vancouver, B.C] 26 Sep 2001: A1 / FRONT.ve

21   Lindsay Kines, Lori Culbert and Kim Bolan. The Vancouver Sun [Vancouver, B.C] 26 Sep 2001: A1 / FRONT.

22   Issues Related to the High Number of Murdered and Missing Women in Canada. http://www.scics.gc.ca/CMFiles/830992005_e1MAJ-2112011-6827.pdf

23   Missing Women Commission of Inquire Consultation Transcripts prepared for the Missing Women Commission of Inquire, February 2012

24   Daily News. Prince Rupert, B.C.: Nov 9, 2006. Pg. 1.Front

25   The Prince George Free Press [Prince George, B.C] 13 Oct 2006: A7.

26   Arthur Williams. Prince George Free Press. Apr 05, 2006

27   RCMP Sergeant Greg Johnson. NCO i/c ViCLAS RCMP Headquarters, Ottawa. RCMP GAZETTE, ViCLAS Violent Crime Linkage Analysis System, Vol. 56, No. 10, 1994

28   http://www.rcmp-grc.gc.ca/gazette/archiv/vol69n1-eng.pdf (Recovered 10/12/2014)

29   http://www.rcmp-grc.gc.ca/gazette/archiv/vol69n1-eng.pdf (Recovered 10/12/2014)

30   Pacific Rate Exchange Service. http://fx.sauder.ubc.ca/etc/GBPpages.pdf (Recovered 10/12/2014)

CHAPTER 8

1   RCMP Gazette, Vol.66, No.3, 2004, Sgt. Matt Logan PhD RCMP Behavioral Science Unit, Vancouver, B.C.

2   Trick, Bernice. Prince George Citizen [Prince George, B.C] 01 Apr 2006: 1 / Front.

3   Debora Tetley. The Calgary Herald. Calgary, Alberta. 01 Mar 2006.

4   Peebles, Frank. Prince George Citizen [Prince George, B.C] 06 Mar 2006: 3.

5   Trick, Bernice. Prince George Citizen [Prince George, B.C] 18 Feb 2006: 13/ .

6   Toronto Star. Toronto. Ont: Mar 3, 2006. Pg A.12

7   Serial Murder: Multi-Disciplinary Perspectives for Investigators: https://www.fbi.gov/stats-services/publications/serial-murder
Pdf Report: https://www.fbi.gov/stats-services/publications/serial-murder/serial-murder-july-2008-pdf

8   Arthur Williams. The Prince George Free Press. Apr. 05, 2006

9   CANILL - Canadian Legal Information Institute. http://canlii.ca/en/sk/skca/doc/2000/2000skca118.htmi [Recovered 09/02/2012]

10   Lakehead University Paleo-dna Laboratory: http://www.ancientdna.com/services.html

11   McMartin, Pete. The Vancouver Sun [Vancouver, B.C] 29 Dec 2012: A.3.

12   Tony Romeyn's original Highway of Tears Web Site, www.highwayoftears.ca, prior to being turned over to the Carrier Sekani Family Services in 2013.

13   Professor of Criminology, Doctor Scott A. Bonn; http://www.docbonn.com/serial-killer-expert.html

14   Forsyth, Bruce, Canadian military history, Canadian Forces Station Baldy Hughes. http://militarybruce.com/abandoned-canadian-military-bases/pinetree-line/admin-3/ [Accessed 10 Nov 2014]

15 Recorded Witness Statement of Leland Switzer taken at Moose Lake Lodge, Prince George, B.C. on Tuesday, August 31st, 2004 at 13:32 hours by Sergeant Bruce Ward of the Criminal Investigation Unit, Major Crime Section, "E" Division R.C.M.P. RCMP File: 2004E-4927.

16 Remington, Robert. Search area 'like something out of Deliverance' Calgary Herald [Calgary, Alta] 29 Aug 2009: A.3 [Accessed 10 Nov 2014]

17 Recorded Witness Statement of Leland Switzer taken at Moose Lake Lodge, Prince George, B.C. on Tuesday, August 31st, 2004 at 13:32 hours by Sergeant Bruce Ward of the Criminal Investigation Unit, Major Crime Section, "E" Division R.C.M.P. RCMP File: 2004E-4927.

18 https://eservice.ag.gov.bc.ca/cso/esearch/criminal/partySearch.

19 Phillips, Bill. The Prince George Free Press [Prince George, B.C] 01 Sep 2009: .8.

20 Williams, Arthur. The Prince George Free Press [Prince George, B.C] 01 Sep 2009: A.1.

21 O'Connor, Elaine. The Province [Vancouver, B.C] 03 Nov 2013: A.3.

22 Jason van Rasel, Calgary Herald, August 20, 2014 06:58AM http://www.princegeorgecitizen.com/news/local-news/killer-linked-to-highway-of-tears-denied-parole-1.1320962

23 Canadian Press NewsWire. Province hires polygraph expert to write report [on accuracy of device after using it to clear youth centre employees] [Toronto] 21 Sep 1997: n/a.

24 Royal Canadian Mounted Police Polygraph Services. http://www.rcmp-grc.gc.ca/ns/prog_services/specialized-services-services-specialises/polygraph-eng.htm [Accessed 11 Nov 2014]

25 Canadian Press NewsWire. Jury still out on polygraph tests [Toronto] 11 Sep 1996: n/a.

26 Missing Women Commission of Inquiry, Vancouver, BC. May 23, 2012 (PROCEEDINGS RESUMED AT 9:32 A.M.) [Accessed 11 Nov 2014]

27 Jason van Rassel, Calgary Herald. August 18, 2014

CHAPTER 9

1 "Drugs and violence in the Hood," Vancouver Sun September 25, 2010, http://www.canada.com/story.html?id=87b02461-26d3-4872-bf48-7aa7666becab [Accessed on October 19, 2014]

2 http://www.pgfreepress.com/taking-back-the-hood/

3 http://www.canada.com/story.html?id=87b02461-26d3-4872-bf48-7aa7666becab

4 The Highway of Tears Symposium Recommendation Report; Pg.9:

5 Tetley, Deborah. Calgary Herald Mother always fearful of Nicole hitching rides: [Calgary, Alta] 22 July 2002: A1 / FRONT

6 Stanfield, Scott. The Ottawa Citizen. RCMP calls off search for missing tree planter: Mysterious disappearance of Nicole Hoar echoes cases of others who vanished in the area [Ottawa, Ont] 09 July 2002. A4.

7 Deborah Tetley. Calgary Herald. Calgary, Alta.: Mar 15, 2003. Pg. B. 1. FRO

8 Hard Core Tree Planters Web Site: http://hardcoretreeplanters.com [Recovered 16 Nov 2011]

9   By Gisele Winton Sarvis, Special to Postmedia Network Thursday, February 13, 2014 9:36:02 EST AM

10 Skeptiko: Science At The Tipping Point Web Site: http://www.skeptiko.com/83-chris-french-psi-claims

11 Paper presented at the British Association Annual Festival of Science 10 September 1996, University of Birmingham Dr. Christopher French, BA PhD CPsychol FBPsS Department of Psychology, Goldsmiths' College, University of London: http://www.eclipse.co.uk/thoughts/paranormal.htm [Recovered Feb. 26, 2014]

12 Gallup Web Site: http://www.gallup.com/poll/16915/three-four-americans-believe-paranormal.aspx [Retrieved Feb. 27, 2014]

13 Deborah Tetley. Calgary Herald. [Calgary, Alberta] 12 May 2007

14 Prince George Search and Rescue Web Site: http://pgsar.ca [Recovered 07 Apr 2014]

15 Opinion 250 News, Saturday, May 12, 2007 10:39 AM. www.oponion250.com/blog/view/5827/1/searcg+underway+for+clues+in+Nicole+hoar [Recovered 17 May 2007]

16 Frank Peebles. Prince George Citizen. [Prince George, B.C] 14 May 2007. Pg. 1. Front

17 Deborah Tetley. Calgary Herald. [Calgary, Alberta] 12 May 2007

18 The Tribune. [Williams Lake, B.C] 18 May 2007. Pg. 15.

19 Deborah Tetley. Calgary Herald. [Calgary, Alberta] 12 May 2007

CHAPTER 10

1   Anonymous. The Interior News. Victim's family thanks Michalko. Letters to the Editor [Smithers, B.C] 09 Apr 2008: A.5. [Accessed 14 Nov 2014]

2   Trick, Bernice. Prince George Citizen [Prince George, B.C] 18 Feb 2006: 13/. [Recovered 28/10/2011]

3   Missing Women Commission of Inquiry, D.J. Adam (for the Commission) In chief by Ms. Winteringham. Vancouver, BC February 16, 2012 (PROCEEDINGS RECONVENED AT 9:32 A.M.).

4   Library and Archives Canada. Key Findings of the Commission of Inquiry into the investigation of the Bombing of Air India Flight 182. http://epe.lac-bac.gc.ca/100/206/301/pco-bcp/commissions/air_india/2010-07-23/www.majorcomm.ca/en/reports/finalreport/key-findings.pdf [Accessed 30 November 2014]

5   British Columbia, Ministry of Justice, Court Services Online: https://eservice.ag.gov.bc.ca/cso/esearch/criminal/partySearch. [Recovered 03/03/2013]

6   Anonymous. Terrace Standard [Terrace, B.C] 19 Mar 2008: 8.

7   Government of Canada. Justice Laws Web Site: http://laws-lois.justice.gc.ca/eng/acts/c-46/section-139.html [Recovered 6/12/2016]

8   Jensen, Ryan. The Interior News. Who cares who finds them. [Smithers, B.C] 07 May 2008: A.4. [Accessed 29 Dec 2013]

9   Letters to the Editor Anonymous. The Interior News [Smithers, B.C] 16 July 2008: A.5.

10 Bender, Quinn. The Interior News [Smithers, B.C] 14 May 2008: a.1.

11 Bender, Quinn. The Interior News [Smithers, B.C] 14 May 2008: A.1.

12 Anonymous. The Interior News [Smithers, B.C] 09 Apr 2008: A.5.

CHAPTER 11

1   Hunter, Stuart. The Province. 'She's been gone too long':: [Vancouver, B.C] 24 Nov 2005: A3

2   Hunter, Stewart. The Province [Vancouver, B.C] 24 November 2005: A3

3   British Columbia, Canada: Crime Reference List. http://www.lloydthomas.org/BC/BCindex.htm

CHAPTER 12

1   The Vancouver Sun [Vancouver, B.C] 21 Sep1989: C8.

2   Vassallo, James. Daily News [Prince Rupert, B.C] 06 Feb 2004: 1 / Front.

3   Vassallo, James. Daily News [Prince Rupert, B.C] 06 Jul 2006: 1 / Front.

CHAPTER 13

1   Middleton, Greg. The Province [Vancouver, B.C] 11 Jan 1996: A15.

2   Kines, Lindsay. The Vancouver Sun [Vancouver, B.C] 05 Dec 1995: B.1

3   Kines, Lindsay. The Vancouver Sun [Vancouver, B.C] 05 Dec 1995: B.1

4   Jason Proctor, The Province News Paper [Vancouver B.C] 06 Feb 2000

5   Middleton, Greg. The Province [Vancouver, B.C] 11 Jan 1996: A.15

6   Jason Proctor, The Province News Paper [Vancouver B.C] 06 Feb 2000

CHAPTER 14

1   Jonathan Fowlie, Calgary Herald, Calgary, Alta.: Jan 31, 2010, pg. A. 6

2   Michelle Cyr-Whiting, Opinion 250.com http://oponion250.com/blog/view/15505/3rally+renews+call+for+highway+of+tears+ing...2/15/2010

3   Anonymous. Dawson Creek Daily News [Dawson Creek, B.C] 29 Nov 2010: B.1.

4   Missing Women Commission of Inquire Web Site: http://www.missingwomeninquiry.ca/

5   Missing Women Commission of Inquire Web Site Consultation Transcripts prepared for the Missing Women Commission of Inquire, February 2012. http://www.missingwomeninquiry.ca/

6   Affidavit of Gary Bass. May 10, 2012. http://www.missingwomeninquiry.ca/wp content/uploads/2012/05/EXHIBIT-199.pdf

7   Missing Women Commission of Inquire Web Site Consultation Transcripts prepared for the Missing Women Commission of Inquire, February 2012. http://www.missingwomeninquiry.ca/

8   Vancouver—The Globe and Mail. Published Thursday, Nov. 25, 2010 9:54PM EST. Last updated Thursday, Nov. 25, 2010 9:57PM EST

9   Matas, Robert. The Globe and Mail [Toronto, Ont] 29 Sep 2010: A.13. [Accessed 15 Aug 2011]

10 http://www.marketwired.com/press-release/missing-women-commission-inquiry-chief-accuses-government-redwashing-says-commission-1545036.htm: Chief Jackie Thomas VANDERHOOF, BRITISH COLUMBIA--(Marketwire - Aug. 2, 2011)

[11] The Highway of Tears Symposium Recommendation Report, June 16, 2006 by when the Lheidi T'enneh Frist Nation, Carrier Sekani Family Services, Carrier Sekani Tribal Council, Prince George Friendship Centre and the Prince George Nechako Aboriginal Employment & Training Association.

[12] Missing Women Commission of Inquiry. STANDING TOGETHER AND MOVING FORWARD: Report on the Pre-Hearing Conference in Prince George and the Northern Community Forum. A CONSULTATION REPORT PREPARED FOR THE MISSING WOMEN COMMISSION OF INQUIRY FEBRUARY 2012 http://www.missingwomeninquiry.ca/wp-content/uploads/2010/10/Report-on-the-Pre-Hearing-Conference-in-Prince-George-and-the-Northern-Community-Forums-00263779.pdf

[13] The Canadian Press Uber Vancouver to get undercover government checks to enforce taxi regulations. Plainclothes agents will pose as potential customers, says B.C. Transportation Minister Todd Stone Posted: Nov 03, 2014 7:31 AM PT | Last Updated: Nov 03, 2014 8:50 PM PT http://www.cbc.ca/news/canada/british-columbia/uber-vancouver-to-get-undercover-government-checks-to-enforce-taxi-regulations-1.2821811 [Accessed 26 November 2014]

[14] The Georgia Straight Web Site, Yolande Cole on Dec 17, 2012 at 1:52 pm: http://www.straight.com/news/wally-oppal-identifies-blatant-police-failures-bcmissing-women-inquiry-report [Recovered 17 December 2012]

[15] Forsaken The Report of the Missing Women Commission of Inquiry. Volume III. The Honourable Wally T. Oppal, QC. Commissioner. British Columbia, November 15, 2012 http://www2.gov.bc.ca/assets/gov/law-crime-and-justice/about-bc-justice-system/inquiries/forsaken-vol_3.pdf

[16] Cameron A. Ward & Company, Barristers & Solicitors Web Site: http://www.cameronward.com/category/news/mwci/ posted by Cameron Ward [Recovered 12 Jun 2016]

[17] Shirley Bond British Columbia Ministry of Justice. http://www2.news.gov.bc.ca/news_releases_2009-2013/2012JAG0324-002043.htm [Accessed 30 November 2015]

[18] Andrea Woo. The Globe and Mail. Pickton lawsuits lead Steven Point to quit women's safety committee, Published Friday, May. 17 2013, 2:59 PM EDT Last updated Friday, May. 17 2013, 3:40 PM EDT http://www.theglobeandmail.com/news/british-columbia/pickton-lawsuits-lead-steven-point-to-quit-womens-safety-committee/article11995544/ [Accessed 30 November 2014]

[19] Jonathan Fowlie. The Vancouver Sun, Capital Daily. Steven Point can bill up to $220,000 as government champion on missing women. March, 2013. 11:57AM. http://blogs.vancouversun.com/2013/03/01/steven-point-can-bill-up-to-220000-as-government-champion/ [Accessed 30 November 2014]

CHAPTER 15

[1] Court of Appeals of Washington, Division 1. STATE of Washington, Respondent, v. Atif Ahmad RAFAY, Appellant. State of Washington, Respondent, v. Glen Sebastian Burns, Appellant. Nos. 55217–1–I, 55218–0–I, 57282–2–I, 57283–1–I. June 18, 2012. http://www.reid.com/pdfs/summer2012/rafay.pdf [Accessed 18 Nov 2014]

[2] Royal Canadian Mounted Police Web Site: http://bc.cb.rcmp-grc.gc.ca/ [Recovered 30 Mar 2014]

[3] Neal Hall, Vancouver Sun Dec 12, 2009: www.vancouversun.com [Recovered 17 Jan 2014]

⌐ er, Vancouver Province: Friday, November 13, 2009

dian Mounted Police in BC Web Site: http://bc.rcmp-grc.gc.ca/ViewPage.ac deId=50&contentId=27095 [Recovered 17 Jan 2014]

CHAPTER 16

1   James Proctor, The Province News Paper [Vancouver B.C] 06 Feb 2000

2   Missing Women Commission of Inquire Transcripts prepared for the Missing Women Commission of Inquire, February 2012. http://www.missingwomeninquiry.ca/

3   Missing Women Commission of Inquire Transcripts prepared for the Missing Women Commission of Inquire, February 2012. http://www.missingwomeninquiry.ca/

4   Missing Women Commission of Inquire Transcripts prepared for the Missing Women Commission of Inquire, February 2012. http://www.missingwomeninquiry.ca/

5   Missing Women Commission of Inquire Transcripts prepared for the Missing Women Commission of Inquire, February 2012. http://www.missingwomeninquiry.ca/

6   Jonathan Fowlie. The Vancouver Sun. Friday, January 30, 2009. www.canada.com [recovered 1/30/2009

7   The Canadian Press Posted: Oct, 2007 1:19 PM Last Updated Oct 01, 2007 6:49 PM ET

8   Royal Canadian Mounted Police Web Site: http://www.rcmp-grc.gc.ca/about-ausujet/organi-eng.htm [Recovered 18 Mar 2014]

9   Family Homes on Reserves and Matrimonial Interests or Rights Act https://www.aadnc aandc.gc.ca/eng/1100100032553/1100100032557

10 Interim Report of the Standing Senate Committee On Human Rights http://www.parl.gc.ca/Content/SEN/Committee/372/huma/10app2-e.pdf

11 Violence in the Lives of Sexually Exploited Youth and Adult Sex Workers in BC Provincial Research. Final Report 2006. Prepared by Sarah Hunt for the Justice Institute of British Columbia, Centre for Leadership and Community Learning

12 Oxman-Martinez, J., et al. 2005. Victims of trafficking in persons: Perspectives from the Canadian community service sector (section 1.1, p. 2). Research and Statistics Division, Department of Justice Canada. Online at: www.canada.justice.gc.ca/eng/pi/rs/rep-rap/2006/rr06_3/toctdm.html.

13 Mary Ellen Turpel-Lafond Representative for Children and Youth—Special Report: When Talk Trumped Service: November 2013

14 British Columbia's Provincial Domestic Violence Plan, Prepared by the Provincial Office of Domestic Violence, February 2014

15 http://www.nwac.ca/wp-content/uploads/2015/05/Fact_Sheet_Violence_Against_Aboriginal_Women.pdf

16 Keller, James. The Canadian Press [Toronto] 13 June 2014.

17 Brian Morton, Vancouver Sun [Vancouver, B.C] 13 Feb 2014. www.vancouversun.com/news [Recovered 06 Apr 2014]

18 Office of The Information & Privacy Commissioner for British Columbia Web Site: https://www.oipc.bc.ca/public-comments/1611 [Recovered 12 Jun 2016]

19 Trinh Theresa Do, CBC News: RCMP confirm report of more than 1,000 murdered aboriginal women. Aboriginal women make up 4 per cent of population, but 16 per cent of all murdered females. Posted: May 02, 2014 8:55 PM ET | Last Updated: May 02, 2014 10:37 PM ET [Recovered 16 Nov 2014]

20 The Highway of Tears Symposium Recommendation Report, June 16, 2006 by when the Lheidi T'enneh Frist Nation, Carrier Sekani Family Services, Carrier Sekani Tribal Council, Prince George Friendship Centre and the Prince George Nechako Aboriginal Employment & Training Association.

21 Babbage, Maria. The Canadian Press. [Toronto, Ontario] 22 Aug 2014.

22 Gloria Galloway, The Globe and Main [Toronto, Ont] April 9, 2015

23 Jackie Hansen and Craig Benjamin. http://www.amnesty.ca/blog/what-happened-at-the-national-roundtable-on-missing-and-murdered-indigenous-women-and-girls. March 1, 2015. Recovered November 8, 2015.

24 Missing Women Commission of Inquire Transcripts prepared for the Missing Women Commission of Inquire, February 2012. http://www.missingwomeninquiry.ca/